Monarch As

NIGEL RICHARDSON

AIRLINES SERIES, VOLUME 15

Front cover image: Airbus A320-200 G-ZBAA on final approach to Palma Airport, Mallorca, June 2013. (Ken Fielding, distributed under a Creative Commons CC BY-SA 3.0 Licence)

Title page image: Airbus A321-231 G-OZBR departing Malaga Airport (Maarten Visser, distributed under a Creative Commons CC BY-SA 2.0 Licence)

Contents page image: Boeing 757-200 G-MONK at Manchester Airport in June 2014. (Nigel Richardson)

Back cover image: Airbus A330-200 G-SMAN at Manchester in July 2014. (Nigel Richardson)

Acknowledgements

I would like to thank the following photographers and organisations for kindly allowing the use of their images in this book, either directly or through Wikimedia Commons/Creative Commons: Aero Icarus, James Abbott, aeroprints.com, Pedro Aragão, Arpingstone, Alex Beltyukov, David Caldwell, Piergiuliano Chesi, Chris from Poznań, John Coleman/ABPic, Terry Dann, Nigel K Daw, DMK Photos, Ken Fielding, Fireballoons, FotoNoir, Erik Frikke, Chris Globe, Geoff Goodall, Lewis Grant, Udo Haafke, Rob Hodgkins, Hullie, Norbert Kröpfl, Stephan Barth Collection, David Mangham, Tony Merton Jones, Andy Mitchell, David A Montgomery, Jonathan Palombo, PropFreak, Riik@mctr, Eric Salard, Robbie Shaw, Björn Strey, Craig Sunter, Andrew Thomas, David Unsworth, Richard Vandervord, John Visanich, Maarten Visser, Lothar Weber, wiltshirespotter, Alan Wilson, Alec Wilson.

I would like to thank my wife, Gill, for proofreading each chapter of the book. Finally, my thanks to Brianne Bellio and her colleagues at Key Publishing.

Published by Key Books
An imprint of Key Publishing Ltd
PO Box 100
Stamford
Lincs PE9 1XQ

www.keypublishing.com

The right of Nigel Richardson to be identified as the author of this book has been asserted in accordance with the Copyright, Designs and Patents Act 1988 Sections 77 and 78.

Copyright © Nigel Richardson, 2023

ISBN 978 1 80282 577 0

Typeset by SJmagic DESIGN SERVICES, India.

Contents

Introduction

International tourism was one of the fastest post-World War Two growth industries until the 1980s. An important part of this growth, especially in Europe, was the development of the inclusive tour (IT), better known as the 'package holiday'. Package holidays were offered for a number of years before the War by tour operators such as Thomas Cook, Inghams and the Travel Club of Upminster, using coach and railway as the usual mode of transport, but the main period of growth in the UK began in 1948.

Initially, inclusive tours were mainly organised for specialist or affinity groups, such as club members, student trips and family reunions, where the tour had a specific purpose other than tourist travel. The start of inclusive holidays by air is often attributed to Vladimir Raitz, who established Horizon Holidays and began running tours to Corsica in 1950, with accommodation in a tented camp. The air travel was contracted to non-scheduled, independent airlines. The number of these charter carriers grew rapidly during the 1950s, mainly due to an abundance of surplus aircraft available at very low prices after the war and the large number of ex-Air Force aircrew available in the labour market. Gradually, the price of inclusive tours began to fall and the public became better aware that package holidays were a relatively cheap and convenient way of enjoying a foreign holiday, with travel agents selling the full tour package.

Although the growth of independent airlines specialising in charter flights for package holidays posed a potential threat to scheduled flag carriers such as British European Airways (BEA), even these airlines benefited from the expansion of international tourism; BEA carried more inclusive tour passengers on scheduled services than the whole of the independent sector did on charter flights. Scheduled airlines also offered more competitive terms to travel agents and tour operators for the use of their flights as part of the holiday package, the so-called ITX fares (inclusive tour excursion fares). Ultimately, this led to a decline in the number of inclusive tour passengers carried by independent airlines in the late 1950s and early 1960s (in 1960–61, British carrier ITX flights exceeded inclusive tour charter flights by almost 35 per cent). Independent charter airlines were also impacted by the Civil Aviation (Licensing) Act (1960), which required UK airlines to have an Air Operator's Certificate (AOC) before they could carry fare-paying passengers and a B Licence for inclusive tour charter flights. The approval process for the operating licence by the newly formed Air Transport Licensing Board (ATLB) was lengthy and time-consuming, involving a rigorous investigation of an airline's financial resources. The first licences were awarded at the beginning of 1962, with more applications initially rejected than accepted. In response, tour operators often contracted their flights to foreign airlines to avoid delays, which also had an impact on charter carriers in the UK. Foreign operators were less likely to have a licence application refused by a government department, as this might result in reciprocal action by the airline's government against a British carrier. In 1962 and 1963, over one-third of such flights between the UK and Europe were provided by foreign airlines.

The sluggishness and unpredictability of the licensing process, together with competition from foreign airlines and the increasing number of UK independent airlines, which led to some severe price cutting, resulted in the financial collapse of several independent carriers. Some airlines experienced such rapid growth that they became financially unstable and collapsed, leaving thousands of passengers stranded abroad. As a consequence, the ATLB increased its scrutiny of the financial standing of UK airlines, further delaying the licensing process. Tour operators, which had also suffered significant financial losses, began to re-evaluate the concept of inclusive tour charters.

Universal Sky Tours, Britain's largest tour operator in the 1950s, specialised in package holidays by air, but made significant losses between 1958 and 1961 from the failures of independent airlines. In an attempt to determine how to resolve future problems, Sky Tours worked in association with aviation consultants. The outcome of their study proposed that an airline should be established, which was almost completely owned by the tour operator, so that flights and tours were integrated and in close working association, and that the airline should specialise almost exclusively in inclusive tour charter flights.

One of the first charter airlines to be established along the lines of these recommendations was Euravia in 1961, which formed a close association with Universal Sky Tours. The airline was renamed Britannia Airways in 1964 and became the charter operator for Thomson Holidays. The early success of Britannia Airways and its rapid expansion of inclusive tour operations encouraged the establishment of other airlines specialising in the provision of charter flights specifically for package holidays. One such airline was Monarch Airlines, formed in 1967 by two former directors of British Eagle Airlines and supported by the large Cosmos Tours holiday group.

This book recounts the history of Monarch Airlines, including its expansion during the 1970s to become one of the UK's largest charter airlines by the early 1980s, meeting the increasing demands of the growing holiday industry. In 1986, Monarch began to operate scheduled flights, but it wasn't until the early to mid-2000s that it experienced significant growth in passenger numbers on these scheduled services. The company's transition from charter airline to predominantly scheduled operator evolved gradually, confirmed by a change in business strategy in 2011, and completed following a decision in 2015 to be an entirely scheduled low-cost carrier. Unfortunately, financial problems ensued and Monarch ceased operations in 2017.

Chapter 1

The Beginning (1967–69)

Monarch Airlines was founded by Bill Hodgson and Don Peacock, directors and businessmen of British Eagle International Airlines (1948–68). Both were aware of growing financial problems at British Eagle and left their positions to establish their own aircraft engineering, maintenance and overhaul company. They aimed to provide a service for smaller, independent airlines that used Bristol Britannia aircraft but didn't have their own engineering resources to undertake any required maintenance work. Hodgson and Peacock established Airline Engineering Ltd in January 1967, with Hodgson becoming Managing Director and Peacock taking the role of Technical Director. From communication with prospective airline customers and drawing on their own knowledge and experiences at British Eagle, the duo became increasingly aware that existing airlines could not provide sufficient seating capacity to meet the needs of the expanding inclusive tour holiday market.

During the 1950s and '60s, there was significant growth in inclusive package holidays, especially to the Mediterranean. State airlines largely concentrated on scheduled services, so it was left to independent airlines to provide charter flights for tour operators in what became the lucrative business of transporting holiday makers to tourism hotspots and other desirable holiday destinations. Independent charter airlines began to establish financial relationships with tour operators, with partnerships that benefited both parties. The tour operators negotiated a preferential price for a guaranteed block of seats on flights, with the airline gaining some financial security from the investment to develop its fleet of aircraft, staffing resources and infrastructure. This process, known as vertical integration, led to the establishment of formal collaborations between airlines and tour operators and sometimes involved charter airlines setting up their own tour operator subsidiary companies.

Cosmos Tours (now Cosmos) is a UK independent tour operator, which is part of the Globus Travel Group, originally formed in 1928 by Swiss Italian, Antonio Mantegazza. He started a company called Globus Viaggi with headquarters in Lugano, Switzerland, that used a fleet of 12 coaches to provide local excursions for European tourists. Gradually the company evolved and started providing overnight excursions to the Dolomites, Venice, Rome and the French Riviera during the 1950s, followed by more regular, longer duration tours in Europe. Cosmos Tours in the UK was founded in 1961 by Antonio's son, Sergio Mantegazza. Initially, Cosmos Tours organised package holidays to Europe for British customers via coach travel from London Victoria Station. However, the tour operator quickly realised the potential of package holidays by air, organising flights from Southend and Lympne airports to destinations in Austria, Italy, Spain and Switzerland.

In 1967, Cosmos Tours was looking for additional seating capacity on flights for its 1968 summer programme. Hodgson and Peacock entered into negotiations with Cosmos and reached a substantial block-booking agreement to provide the required seats, establishing Monarch Airlines Ltd on 1 June 1967. However, after considering their operational costs and proposed schedules, and reviewing their business plans, Hodgson and Peacock concluded that the company's available working capital would only sustain the airline for one year of operations. Armed with this information, they approached Cosmos again and, after further discussion, Cosmos Tours agreed to provide 80 per cent of the finance required to support the airline in its early years. Monarch was operated as a subsidiary of Globus Getaway Holdings. Captain AJ Burridge was appointed as Chief Pilot and ES Wright as the company's Operations Manager in early 1968, followed by the recruitment of eight flight crews. The Monarch Airlines-Cosmos Tours pairing was to become a good example of vertical integration.

Following the establishment of Monarch Airlines, the next stage was to identify a base from which to operate. A location in the south of England was favoured. Heathrow Airport didn't handle inclusive tour flights and there was no suitable space at Gatwick, so the choice was Stansted or Luton. Ultimately Luton Airport was selected because it had adequate space to accommodate the airline and two vacant hangars for the airline's engineering business. Luton was already a popular airport for thousands of British holidaymakers and had good road links from London, the south of England and the Midlands, encompassing a catchment population of approximately 20 million people. Modifications to the hangar space were essential to accommodate at least two aircraft at a time. The local council, Luton Corporation, was actively encouraging expansion at their airport and contributed a grant of £60,000 towards the cost of the hangar refurbishment.

Monarch's first aircraft were two Bristol 175 Britannia 300s (G-AOVI and G-AOVH) acquired from Caledonian Airways, which was replacing its Britannia fleet with Boeing 707s and BAC One-Elevens. The Britannia, known as the 'whispering giant' for its quiet exterior noise and smooth flying, was powered by four Bristol Proteus 765 turboprop engines. The Series 300 aircraft was the largest variant of the Bristol Britannia, with a fuselage length of 37.9m. The first Britannia acquired by Monarch was G-AOVI. It was transported from Gatwick Airport to Southend in January 1968 before transfer to Marshalls at Cambridge for an overhaul, painting and fitting out to Monarch's requirements. Airline Engineering Ltd was not yet sufficiently established to complete this work. The aircraft cabin was fitted with 143 seats in a single-class tourist configuration, and the aircraft was painted in a yellow, white and black livery. G-AOVI moved to Monarch's Luton base on 8 March 1968 and completed a proving flight from Luton to Rome on 15 March. The aircraft was leased back to Caledonian Airways to transport pilgrims to Mecca during the annual Hajj festival in advance of its final delivery to Monarch at Luton Airport on 4 April

Bristol Britannia 312 G-AOVI was the first Britannia to be acquired by Monarch in March 1968. (John Coleman/ABPic)

Bristol Britannia 312 G-AOVH at Manchester in April 1971. (Ken Fielding, distributed under a Creative Commons CC BY-SA 3.0 Licence)

Bristol Britannia 309 G-ANCH was acquired by Monarch in October 1968. It is shown here in storage at Lydd after being withdrawn from service in April 1972. (Tony Merton Jones)

Bristol Britannia 308F G-ANCF at Luton Airport in April 1974. (John Coleman/ABPic)

Bristol Britannia 312 G-AOVL was acquired by Monarch in March 1969. It is seen here at Palma Airport, Mallorca, in July 1969. (Erik Frikke)

1968. The second Britannia, G-AOVH, was handed over to Monarch on 1 April 1968 and, following a similar overhaul and preparation programme by Marshalls, was delivered from Cambridge to Luton on 20 April 1968.

Monarch's inaugural revenue service took place on 5 April 1968 – an inclusive tour charter from Luton to Madrid, flown by Britannia G-AOVI. This was followed by an ad hoc charter from Luton to Rotterdam on 17 April. However, for much of April, the Britannias were involved in crew training.

During the summer of 1968, Monarch's Britannia fleet was almost exclusively contracted by Cosmos to operate inclusive tour flights from Luton to a number of European destinations including Barcelona, Bordeaux, Basle, Gerona, Ibiza, Madrid, Malaga, Palma, Rimini, Valencia and Venice. The airline also undertook a small number of ad hoc passenger charters for other airlines, including from Gatwick to Las Palmas on behalf of British United Airways, and from Stansted to Palma and Genoa for Channel Airways. Some charters were operated for the Ministry of Defence (MoD), transporting service personnel and their families from Luton to bases in Aden and Gütersloh and Wildenrath in West Germany. A third Britannia, G-ANCH, was acquired on a long-term lease from Ghana Airways, entering service in October 1968 when it flew an MoD charter from Luton to Aden.

On 6 November 1968, British Eagle ceased trading before going into liquidation two days later. Three former British Eagle Bristol Britannias eventually joined the Monarch fleet, together with a number of that airline's employees. The first aircraft acquired from British Eagle's liquidators and delivered to Monarch in early December 1968 was G-ANCF. This aircraft was particularly valuable since it was a convertible passenger/freight aircraft, fitted with a large cargo door. In November 1968, Monarch had been awarded a contract from the Ministry of Technology and Ministry of Defence to transport equipment and personnel for weapons development and testing at the Woomera rocket test range in South Australia. A proving flight was completed in late November of that year by G-ANCF, preceding a regular, fortnightly service, with an inaugural flight from Luton on 18 December 1968. The service, previously flown by British Eagle, usually operated from RAF Lyneham or RAF Brize Norton, with flights to both Perth and Adelaide. Some of Monarch's other Britannia aircraft (G-AOVH, G-AOVT, G-ANCE) contributed to the scheduled operations until the final service, which took place on 15 December 1975.

The prestigious and lucrative Australia contract formalised further MoD charter work involving the transport of military personnel from Birmingham, Edinburgh, Manchester and Teeside airports to British bases in West Germany, including Berlin, Dusseldorf, Gütersloh and Hannover, with occasional flights to Akrotiri in Greece and to Gibraltar.

Monarch's 1968–69 winter season included new holiday routes from Luton to Tenerife in the Canary Isles, Munich (for skiing holidays) and the Far East. By the end of 1968, Monarch had transported nearly 123,000 passengers in just nine months of operation.

By the start of the 1969 summer season, Monarch had acquired two more former British Eagle Bristol Britannias (G-AOVL and G-AOVT) for passenger services, and two additional aircraft were purchased to be dismantled for spares to keep the Britannia fleet flying. For most of the year, the fleet of six aircraft was used largely on Cosmos holiday tour charters from Luton, although other tour work and an increasing amount of ad hoc charter work was undertaken in both passenger and freight configurations, including some flights from Manchester and Gatwick. The summer inclusive tour charter programme was more extensive than in the previous year and included new services to Athens, Faro, Genoa, Mahón, Pisa, Tenerife, and Tunis as well as those destinations offered during the summer of 1968. Additional winter season services included flights to Alicante, Rhodes and Tarbes. Monarch also became involved with the Hajj pilgrim flights, flying passengers from Africa and the Middle East to and from Jeddah. Almost 269,000 passengers were carried aboard Monarch's aircraft during 1969, the airline's first complete year of operations.

Bristol Britannia 308F G-ANCF at Bahrain International Airport, Muharraq, September 1970. (Robbie Shaw)

Bristol Britannia 312 G-AOVG at Milan Linate Airport in August 1973. (Piergiuliano Chesi, distributed under a Creative Commons CC BY 3.0 Licence)

Bristol Britannia 312 G-AOVN at Munich Airport, October 1973, on one of her last Monarch flights before retirement in November 1973. (Norbert Kröpfl, Stephan Barth Collection)

Above: Bristol Britannia 312 G-AOVG was acquired by Monarch in October 1969 and operated for the carrier for just over 4 years. She is seen here at Luton Airport in April 1973. (Terry Dann)

Left: Bristol Britannia 308F G-ANCF at Perth, Australia in February 1974. (Geoff Goodall)

Below: Bristol Britannia 308F G-ANCF at Adelaide Airport, April 1972, following a Weapons Research Establishment courier flight. (Nigel K. Daw)

Bristol Britannia 312 G-AOVT on display at the Imperial War Museum, Duxford, Cambridgeshire. (Alan Wilson, distributed under a Creative Commons CC BY-SA 2.0 Licence)

Above left: The passenger cabin of Bristol Britannia G-AOVT, showing the 3+3 seating configuration. (David Unsworth)

Above right: Front cover of Monarch Airlines' Flight Souvenir magazine. (Author's Collection)

Chapter 2

Over to Jets (the 1970s)

At the beginning of the 1970 summer programme, Monarch had eight Bristol Britannias in service. Two more aircraft (G-AOVG and G-AOVN) had joined the fleet at the end of 1969. The airline was actively providing contract charter flights for Cosmos's expanded tour programme, which now included holiday destinations in North Africa, Portugal and Yugoslavia. Monarch's services from Luton included Athens, Barcelona, Basle, Faro, Genoa, Ibiza, Madrid, Mahón, Malaga, Milan, Palma, Pisa, Rimini, Split, Tenerife, Tunis, Valencia and Venice.

From April 1970, Monarch branched out with another tour operator, the Clarksons Travel Group, undertaking contract work at an airport other than Luton for the first time. The contract for Clarksons was to carry passengers on day-trip and short-stay charters from Manchester to Beauvais in France for excursions to Paris, and Manchester to Rotterdam to visit the Dutch bulb fields. Monarch's Britannias also flew Clarksons Tours from Luton to both Beauvais and Rotterdam.

Monarch's operations remained relatively unchanged during 1971, a year when the airline began to evaluate several different types of jet aircraft. While the turboprop Bristol Britannias were proving to be excellent, versatile aircraft, which had fulfilled the needs of the airline for the past three years, they were ageing and would soon require a major overhaul or replacement. Monarch required jets that could match the operational flexibility of the Britannia in flying both short- and medium-range routes. An alternative approach would have been to develop two fleets of jet aircraft, one with short-range capability and the other for medium- to long-range services. Jet aircraft available at the time included the de Havilland Comet, Douglas DC-9 and the BAC One-Eleven, all of which were highly competitive economically for inclusive tour operations. At Boeing, the options included the Boeing 720, a short- to medium-range version of the Boeing 707, which had been in service since 1960, and the Boeing 737 Original Series, launched in 1965, which had recently entered service with Lufthansa in 1968. While serious consideration was given to the BAC One-Eleven, noise restrictions on night flying by jets led Monarch to enter the jet age using the Boeing 720B, as it could carry more passengers on each night jet movement, and operational costs were similar to those of the One-Eleven. The aircraft was an improved variant of the original Boeing 720, with four Pratt & Whitney JT3D turbofan engines, a range of up to 3,200nm and initially configured to accommodate 131–137 passengers in two classes, or 156 passengers in a single class seating configuration.

Monarch acquired its first three Boeing 720Bs from Northwest Orient. The first aircraft (G-AZFB) was handed over at a ceremony in Minneapolis in September 1971. It was delivered to Luton on 28 November that year after undergoing a number of modifications, including the fitting of a high-density seating configuration to accommodate up to 170 passengers and the addition of extra emergency exits. The aircraft obtained its Certificate of Airworthiness on 11 December 1971 and, two days later, completed Monarch's first 720B service from Luton to Tunis. Two more Boeing 720Bs were delivered in January and March 1972. Monarch's introduction of jets into its aircraft fleet was marked by the launch of a revised livery comprising a grey fuselage underbelly separated from a white upper fuselage and vertical stabiliser by yellow-and-black cheatlines.

The introduction of the Boeing 720B led to the retirement of four Britannias in May 1972. The leased Britannia from Ghana Airways (G-ANCH) flew its final service for Monarch on 30 April 1972. The two founder members of the fleet, G-AOVH and G-AOVI were retired together with G-AOVL. Therefore,

The first Boeing 720B G-AZFB to be acquired by Monarch. The aircraft was handed over in September 1971 followed by delivery in November 1971, after undergoing some modifications. (Ken Fielding, distributed under a Creative Commons CC BY-SA 3.0 Licence)

Boeing 720B G-AZNX taxiing for departure at East Midlands Airport. (Rob Hodgkins, distributed under a Creative Commons CC BY-SA 2.0 Licence)

Get into Europe the 720B way

We know that you are all enthusiasts and will know that Monarch is the only British airline which operates the fabulous Boeing 720B aircraft. The best way to get to know more about the aircraft is to fly in it. We fly most of Cosmos Tours holiday clients from Luton to Spain, Italy, the Canary Islands, Tunisia, Greece, Yugoslavia and Portugal, and holidays start at £16.50 for a four day Funbreak in Lloret. So call in at your Travel Agent and book a Cosmos 720B holiday.

MONARCH AIRLINES LIMITED
Luton Airport Luton Beds. LU2 9NU
Tel: Luton 27151
Cables: Monarch Luton.
Telex No. 82440

COSMOS TOURS LIMITED
Cosmos House
1 Bromley Common
Bromley, Kent.
BR2 9LX.
Tel: 01-464 3444

Above: Boeing 720B G-AZKM was the second B720 to be acquired by Monarch. It is shown here taxiing at Manchester Airport. (Andrew Thomas, distributed under a Creative Commons CC BY-SA 2.0 Licence)

Left: A magazine advertisement promoting the introduction of the Boeing 720B into Monarch's fleet (Author's Collection)

at the start of the 1972 summer season, Monarch's fleet consisted of four Britannias and three 'new' Boeing 720Bs. With Britannia G-ANCF mainly operating the MoD freight flights to Australia, the three remaining Britannias were generally used on shorter-range, inclusive tour charter routes, including to Barcelona, Basle, Dubrovnik, Faro, Gerona, Ibiza, Malaga, Mahón, Naples, Palma, Pisa, Rimini, Split and Venice.

The Boeing 720Bs were initially flown on Monarch's high-density passenger routes from Luton to Alicante, Gerona, Palma and Ibiza, and on long distance-services to Las Palmas, Tenerife, Cyprus, and various destinations in Greece, including Athens and Rhodes. They were also involved with ad hoc charter flights to European destinations, often from Birmingham and other regional airports. By the end of the year the Boeing 720Bs had taken over most of Monarch's passenger services. Director Bill Hodgson was impressed with the performance and efficiency of the 720B, and particularly the low noise levels, referring to the aircraft as 'whispering giants', a label previously assigned to the Bristol Britannia. Several of the 720Bs flew services from London Heathrow on behalf of BOAC during 1973 due to a temporary shortage of aircraft at BOAC.

Monarch carried 529,000 passengers in 1972, the first time it had exceeded the half-million total.

Monarch's associate company, Airline Engineering Ltd, played a key role in overhauling the Britannias and ensuring that sufficient numbers of aircraft were always serviceable. The company also undertook maintenance work on Britannias from other airlines. Such third-party work had been the primary aim of the company when it was established in 1967. Aircraft from African Safari Airways, Cubana, International Air Services and several other airlines were handled by Airline Engineering at this time.

During the 1973 summer season, the Monarch fleet remained unchanged and was supplemented, in September, by the arrival of Bristol Britannia G-ANCE from Lloyd International. The aircraft entered service in November 1973 mainly supporting Britannia G-ANCF on Monarch's UK-Australia MoD service. It was sold to Aer Turas in May 1974.

Just as Monarch Airlines was beginning to expand operations, the Yom Kippur War broke out in October 1973. As a result, the Organisation of Arab Petroleum Exporting Countries (OAPEC) reduced petroleum production and announced an embargo on oil supplies (by as much as 40 per cent) to countries that supported Israel during the war. This resulted in a tripling of the price of aviation fuel in October 1973, followed by a quadrupling by the end of the war in April 1974. The oil crisis contributed to a significant downturn in the UK economy. At the same time, national industrial disputes with coal miners and rail workers resulted in an enforced three-day working week. With increased fuel costs and potential fuel shortages, Monarch, along with other airlines, experienced a period of financial hardship. Surcharges were imposed by the airlines on the tour operators, which were passed on to customers for the price of holidays. As a consequence, there was a significant decline (over 30 per cent) in the number of bookings for holidays abroad for the 1974 summer season.

One airline that suffered irreversibly as a result of the recession was Court Line Aviation. More than 70 per cent of Court Line's charter capacity was contracted by tour operator, Clarksons Holidays. Clarksons was taken over by Court Line in April 1973 following financial difficulties and was on the verge of bankruptcy. In 1974 Court Line acquired the Horizon Holidays Group due to the impact of the recession on holiday bookings. However, Court Line had its own financial problems. The airline had invested heavily in several wide-body Lockheed L-1011 Tristars in 1973, as well as taking on the debts of Clarksons Holidays. It had also been involved in legal disputes with British Caledonian and Thomas Cook following the takeover of Horizon Holidays. Despite the UK government purchasing the company's shipbuilding assets for £60 million in June 1974, Court Line Aviation and its tour companies ceased trading on 15 August 1974. Cosmos Tours seized the opportunity to gain from the demise of one of its rivals and started planning inclusive tours from Bristol Airport beginning in 1975, in the hope of attracting some of Clarksons' former customers. Monarch began negotiations with the British Aircraft Corporation (BAC) to lease two of Court Lines' former BAC One-Elevens to operate Cosmos's planned 1975 summer programme from Bristol.

Monarch reduced its Britannia fleet during the 1973–74 winter season, with G-AOVN withdrawn from service in November 1973, followed by G-AOVG in January 1974. This left just one Britannia (G-AOVT) remaining in Monarch passenger service. This aircraft operated during the 1974 summer season, mainly as back-up to the airline's growing fleet of Boeing 720Bs. On 29 March 1974, Monarch Airlines Ltd and Airline Engineering Ltd were combined into a single company called Cosmos Tours (UK) Ltd.

In March 1974, Monarch acquired its fourth Boeing 720B (G-BBZG) on lease from Maersk Air of Copenhagen. A series of transatlantic flights was flown by the 720Bs from Birmingham to Toronto and Vancouver. Due to the relatively short runway at Birmingham Airport and the limited range of the Boeing 720B, the flights often involved a fuel stop at Gander, Newfoundland. These charter flights, flown on behalf of Solihull Travel Company, began on 14 June 1974 and departed every Friday until 23 August, when the last flight operated by G-AZKM left Birmingham. At this point Solihull Travel Company was experiencing financial difficulties, which put an end to the service.

During August 1974 Monarch flew a number of scheduled services for Iraqi Airways. The flights from London Heathrow to Baghdad were eventually taken over by British Midland at the end of the month.

Monarch's passenger services operated by the Bristol Britannia finally came to an end on 9 October 1974 when G-AOVT flew the last commercial passenger flight from Luton to Basle, Switzerland. However, the aircraft flew a final service for Northeast Airlines on 13 October 1974, from Lisbon to London Heathrow, when it replaced an unserviceable Hawker Siddeley Trident. This flight was particularly significant since it was the final operation of a passenger service by a British-registered Bristol Britannia. Monarch's

Boeing 720B G-BBZG was leased by Monarch from Maersk Air between February 1974 and December 1975. (Udo Haafke)

freight flights to Adelaide for the MoD involving Britannia G-ANCF continued until December 1975 before the aircraft was sold to African Safari Airways.

The impact of the oil crisis and economic recession in the UK was evident in Monarch's passenger numbers for 1974. A total of 505,930 passengers were carried during 1974, a decline of almost 17 per cent compared with the previous year.

The first BAC One-Eleven Series 500 arrived at the end of February 1975, followed by a second aircraft in March of the same year. The One-Eleven made its maiden flight in August 1963. It had been designed for short–medium haul schedules and feeder flights involving short duration turnarounds. Therefore, it was highly suited for Monarch's holiday charters. The Series 500 aircraft was 13ft 6in longer than the Series 200/300/400 aircraft and could accommodate up to 119 passengers. Fitted with more powerful Spey Mk512 engines, it was highly suited to operating from airfields with short runways, such as at Bristol Airport where the Boeing 720B was too large to be used.

The One-Elevens were used for crew training and route familiarisation during March 1975 before entering service, initially flying inclusive tour charters from Luton to various European destinations, although some ad hoc charters were flown from other regional airports. Charter flights from Bristol for Cosmos's new package tours began on 17 May 1975. The summer programme from Bristol was to that company's more popular holiday destinations, including Alicante, Gerona, Ibiza, Palma, Rimini and Venice.

In addition to Bristol, Monarch opened new bases at Birmingham and East Midlands airports, using both Boeing 720B and BAC One-Eleven fleets. Inclusive tour charter services from Birmingham started on 3 April 1975 with a Boeing 720B flying to Monastir, Tunisia. Other destinations from Birmingham throughout the summer of 1975 included Ibiza, Mahón, Milan, Palma, Rome and Treviso. Monarch's first service from East Midlands Airport was to Ibiza on 17 May 1975, flown by Boeing 720B G-AZNX.

An interesting development in 1975 saw Cosmos begin to offer 'seat-only' bookings on Monarch flights to popular holiday destinations. From the mid-1970s, British holidaymakers increasingly wanted to find

BAC 1-11 500 G-BCWG was the first One-Eleven to be operated by Monarch. (David A. Montgomery)

BAC 1-11 500 G-BCXR was acquired by Monarch in March 1975 and went on to operate for the airline until March 1983. (Ken Fielding, distributed under a Creative Commons CC BY-SA 3.0 Licence)

their own accommodation rather than stay in large hotels as part of package holidays. In addition, the rise of the timeshare market meant more people had purchased part-ownership of villas and apartments. Demand grew for flights cheaper than those offered by scheduled airlines and for destinations not served by scheduled carriers. At the time, it was illegal to sell charter flights without accommodation, therefore Cosmos offered packages that included seats on a Monarch charter flight and a voucher for basic accommodation, usually in dormitory-style rooms with no private facilities, which customers could then throw away. A Cosmos package to Greece, for example, which was promoted as a 'cheapie', cost £59, while the most economical British Airways scheduled flight to Athens cost £125 return. However, the seat-only tickets were not widely available and were not offered to all charter flight destinations. And, since they were operated on a charter timetable, they did not provide the levels of consistency and frequency that would be associated with a scheduled service. Nonetheless, it was an initial departure from charter flights being an integral part of an inclusive tour holiday.

Although Monarch was no longer flying Bristol Britannias on passenger services, and had only one of this type remaining in its fleet, its subsidiary Airline Engineering's association with the Britannia didn't end. The company continued to maintain Britannias for other airlines and, following the retirement and disposal of the Royal Air Force's entire fleet of Britannias in the autumn of 1975, it was also responsible for the overhaul and conversion of most of the aircraft, including several of Monarch's former Britannias, for other customers, including Aer Turas of Ireland and Gemini Air Transport of Ghana. Indeed, Airline Engineering continued to maintain and service these aircraft for a number of years.

From November 1975 to January 1976, Monarch wet-leased two Boeing 720Bs to Garuda Indonesia, for use on the annual series of Hajj pilgrim flights to Mecca. A third BAC One-Eleven (G-AWWZ) was acquired in November 1975 to replace one of Monarch's Boeing 720Bs (G-BBZG), which was returned to Maersk Air at the end of the lease period. The One-Eleven went into service on 11 December, operating a charter flight from Luton to Vienna.

The heavy demand for Cosmos holidays during 1975 and the associated expansion of Monarch's domestic presence and charter operations resulted in 778,690 passengers travelling with the airline, an increase of more than 50 per cent compared with the previous year.

At the beginning of 1976, Monarch had a fleet of three BAC One-Elevens and three Boeing 720Bs in service. There was further expansion of the inclusive tour charter programme from Luton to 40 destinations including in France, Greece, Spain, Italy, Portugal, Norway, Yugoslavia, Germany, Austria, Switzerland, Finland and St Lucia. Most of these services were flown by both the One-Elevens and 720Bs, although longer flights to locations such as Athens, Heraklion, Las Palmas, Rhodes, St Lucia, Tenerife and Tunis were flown solely by the Boeing 720Bs. Several charter services for Cosmos were also flown from Birmingham, although services from East Midlands Airport were reduced to just one service per week to Ibiza, which was usually flown by a One-Eleven. Other operations included additional inclusive tour and ad hoc charters, such as Gatwick to Lisbon and Rome. One-Eleven G-BCWG was returned to the lessor in October 1976 and replaced by another One-Eleven, G-AXMG.

In March 1978, Monarch acquired a former American Airlines Boeing 707-123B (G-BMFI) to be used on long-haul inclusive tour flights to St Lucia. The aircraft was sold to Cyprus Airways in January 1979, being replaced by Boeing 707-123B G-BGCT until December 1979 when it was also sold to Cyprus Airways. The number of Boeing 720Bs in the fleet had increased to five following the acquisition of two aircraft in March 1977 and January 1978. A sixth 720B was added in November 1979.

At the end of the decade, Monarch's two founding directors, Bill Hodgson and Don Peacock, stepped down and were replaced by former Dan-Air Managing Director Alan Snudden. The airline achieved an important milestone in Hodgson and Peacock's final year in control, carrying more than one million passengers for the first time.

Right: BAC 1-11 500 G-AWWZ was the last One-Eleven to be operated by Monarch before its withdrawal from service in October 1985. (Richard Vandervord)

Below: Boeing 707-123B G-BFMI is seen here taxiing at Malta International Airport in December 1978. (John Visanich)

BAC 1-11 500 G-AXMG joined Monarch's aircraft fleet in October 1976 to replace 1-11 G-BCWG which returned to the lessor. (Pedro Aragão, distributed under a Creative Commons CC BY-SA 3.0 Licence)

Boeing 707-123B G-BGCT was acquired by Monarch in December 1978, replacing B707-123B G-BFMI. (David Mangham)

Boeing 707-123B G-BGCT at Malta International Airport. (John Visanich)

Boeing 720B G-BCBA was acquired by Monarch in March 1977 and remained in service until October 1981. (John Visanich)

Boeing 720B G-AZFB was one of the last Boeing 720Bs to operate for Monarch (Ken Fielding, distributed under a Creative Commons CC BY-SA 3.0 Licence)

BAC 1-11 500 G-AWWZ at London Gatwick Airport. (Richard Vandervord)

BAC 1-11 500 G-BCWG at Zurich Airport in November 1975. (Aero Icarus, distributed under a Creative Commons CC BY-SA 2.0 Licence)

Monarch Airlines leased Boeing 707-123 G-BHOY from March to May 1980 before the aircraft moved on to Air Malta. (Richard Vandervord)

Chapter 3

Expanding Horizons (1980s and 1990s)

Monarch opened 1980 with an order for a new aircraft, the Boeing 737-200. The Boeing 737 was designed in the 1960s as a short-haul airliner to compete with the BAC One-Eleven and Douglas DC-9. The 737 had been in service with many operators, including a number of charter airlines, for 12 years. The Boeing 737-200 featured a 26in fuselage extension compared to the original -100 series, providing seating for up to 130 passengers in a six-abreast, single class configuration. The 737-200 Advanced variant, ordered by Monarch, had improved aerodynamics, more powerful Pratt & Whitney JT8D-17 turbofan engines and greater fuel capacity, giving a 15 per cent increase in payload and range over the original -200 series. An order was placed for the lease of two aircraft from Bavaria Leasing (a unit of Hapag Lloyd Airlines at the time), together with an option on a third. Monarch received its first aircraft, registered G-DFUB, in September 1980, followed by the second in October of that year (G-BMON). The option for a third Boeing 737-200 was taken up, with G-BJSO arriving in December 1981. Three more aircraft followed between March 1982 and May 1984. One and sometimes both of the first two aircraft were mainly based at Berlin Tegel Airport in the French sector of Berlin, where they operated inclusive tour charter flights to the Mediterranean and Canary Islands under contract to one of West Berlin's leading tour operators, Flug-Union Berlin, from the start of the 1981 summer season. Monarch took over the charter contract from Laker Airways, which had been operating it since 1968.

Following the arrival of the first two Boeing 737-200s, Monarch began to withdraw some of its Boeing 720Bs, selling one aircraft (G-BHGE) to Conair at the beginning of July 1981 and two aircraft (G-BCBA and G-BCBB) to Israeli charter airline Maof at the end of the 1981 summer season. Monarch continued to operate at least one Boeing 707 on its long-haul services at the beginning of the decade, with G-BHOX and G-BHOY used at various times during 1980 and replaced by G-AXRS for 1981.

The first Boeing 737-200 G-DFUB to be received by Monarch was registered as G-DFUB, seen here at Faro in 1985. (Pedro Aragão, distributed under a Creative Commons CC BY-SA 3.0 Licence)

Left: Boeing 737-200 G-BMON at Berlin Tegel Airport in 1982. (Lothar Weber)

Below: Boeing 737-200 G-BJSO was delivered to Monarch in December 1981. (Aero Icarus, distributed under a Creative Commons CC BY-SA 2.0 Licence)

Boeing 737-200 G-DGDP in a hybrid livery at Manchester in July 1984. (Ken Fielding, distributed under a Creative Commons CC BY-SA 3.0 Licence)

Monarch further extended its regional presence in the UK by opening new charter bases at Gatwick, Glasgow and Manchester in 1981. A total of 1,118,655 passengers were transported to and from UK airports by Monarch throughout the year. The airline operated to 75 destinations from the UK during the summer season as well as 17 from Berlin.

Monarch took further steps to expand and modernise its fleet in 1981 by placing an initial order for four Boeing 757-200 aircraft. The airline was the third operator of the 757 after Eastern Airlines and British Airways, and the first charter airline to place an order for the new aircraft type. Although Monarch was now a well-established charter operator with more than 1,000 employees, this was a significant decision for a relatively small airline.

The Boeing 757 originally emerged as the 7N7 concept from Boeing's New Aircraft Programme in the 1970s, the objective of which was to design some 'new generation' airliners to replace its current B707, B727, B737 and B747 aircraft. The 7N7 was a single-aisle, narrow body aircraft. It featured the use of new lighter structural materials such as aluminium alloys and graphite composites, fuel-efficient high-bypass turbofan engines (either the Pratt & Whitney JT10D, later designated the PW 2037, or the Rolls-Royce RB211-535) and a new advanced wing. Together, these technological advances promised a significant reduction in operating costs. The 7N7 was eventually designated the Boeing 757; the first prototype was rolled out of Boeing's Renton site in Washington on 13 January 1982 before making its maiden flight on 19 February 1982, almost a year after Monarch had placed an order for the aircraft. The Boeing 757's unusually high thrust-to-weight ratio means that it is particularly effective at operating out of airports with short runways as well as those affected by hot weather, hence it became known as the 'pocket rocket'. It was these potential performance characteristics, together with the 757's low operating costs and high seating capacity, that were particularly appealing to Monarch.

Alongside the order for the Boeing 757, Monarch placed an order for two Boeing 737-300s. Development of the Classic series or second generation Boeing 737s as an upgrade of the original series started in 1979. The 737-300 was powered by the CFM56-3B-1 high-bypass turbofan engine, which provided a significant improvement in fuel economy and noise reduction. It featured a lengthened fuselage (by 9ft 5in), increasing the passenger capacity to 149, and modifications to the wing to improve aerodynamic performance. The 737-300 prototype first flew in February 1984 and entered service in December that year. Monarch's combined order for four Boeing 757-200s and two Boeing 737-300s was valued at more than £70 million based on list prices at the time. Another 11 737-300s were ordered at a later date.

The first Boeing 757-200 (G-MONB) was delivered to Monarch in March 1983. Its arrival coincided with the introduction of an updated livery, the third in the airline's history. It comprised a grey underbelly, with black-and-yellow cheat lines separating a white upper and lower fuselage and a crown-style logo on the tail. Several more 757s were delivered in April and May 1983 and a fourth aircraft in March 1985. Further fleet changes included the departure of the remaining three Boeing 720Bs in March and April 1983 and the last BAC One-Eleven in October 1985, followed by the delivery of the first three Boeing 737-300s in March and May 1986. By the beginning of the 1986 summer season, Monarch had an 'all Boeing' fleet consisting of three Boeing 737-200s, three Boeing 737-300s and four Boeing 757-200s.

The acquisition of new aircraft required modernisation and expansion of Monarch Aircraft Engineering's facilities at Luton Airport. The former Airline Engineering Ltd. was renamed Monarch Aircraft Engineering Ltd in March 1980. Several new hangars were added in 1986 and two more in 1993. These improvements ensured that Monarch Aircraft Engineering had sufficient space to complete the maintenance and servicing of six aircraft simultaneously.

In 1985, the UK government was advocating greater liberalisation in Europe with regard to the relaxation of licensing regulations on scheduled services, which made it possible for charter airlines to offer flight-only bookings to holiday destinations. In spring 1985, the Civil Aviation Authority (CAA)

Boeing 757-200 G-MONB was the first aircraft of the type to be acquired by Monarch in March 1983. (Aero Icarus, distributed under a Creative Commons CC BY-SA 2.0 Licence)

Boeing 757-200 G-MONC in June 1985. The aircraft is painted in an updated livery which was introduced when Boeing 757s were first delivered to Monarch. (wiltshirespotter, distributed under a Creative Commons CC BY-SA 2.0 Licence)

Boeing 737-300 G-DHSW was the first 737-300 to be acquired by Monarch, following delivery in March 1986. (Pedro Aragão, distributed under a Creative Commons CC BY-SA 3.0 Licence)

Boeing 737-300 G-MONF at Faro in 1989. (Pedro Aragão, distributed under a Creative Commons CC BY-SA 3.0 Licence)

granted Monarch licences to begin scheduled flights from Luton to Malaga, Mahón (Menorca) and Tenerife. These represented Monarch's first scheduled services. Monarch launched its programme of scheduled flights in 1986 under the brand name Monarch Crown Service to distinguish it from its charter operations, which remained branded as Monarch. In order to market the scheduled flights, Monarch formed a subsidiary called Monarch Air Travel. The first scheduled flight was to Mahón on 5 July 1986. The air fare for Crown Service included a four-course meal with wine, hot towels and in-flight entertainment. The airline received further approval, at a later date, for Crown Service flights to Alicante, Gibraltar and Palma, including some services operated from other bases. The new scheduled services became popular and started to impact on Monarch's traditional inclusive tour activities. However, scheduled services marked the first time that Monarch was in direct competition with other airlines on some routes, rather than just as a component of a tour operator.

As the number of Boeing 737-300s in the fleet slowly increased, the last remaining Boeing 737-200 left Monarch in January 1988. On 1 May 1988, Monarch entered the long-haul market, operating the first ETOPS 120-minutes rule transatlantic operation under CAA regulations. ETOPS or Extended-range Twin-engine Operations Performance Standards under the 120-minutes rule is an approval given by a regulatory body, such as the CAA, that permits twin-engine aircraft to operate in airspace or along a route no more than 120 minutes flying time from a diversion airfield at an approved one-engine inoperative cruise speed, over water or remote land areas. Monarch was the first British airline to be certified for ETOPS operations by the CAA. Boeing 757-200ER G-MONT operated between Luton and Orlando, via Gander, Newfoundland, carrying 235 passengers. The flight was the first ever British-operated twin-jet to cross the Atlantic with passengers, and was Monarch's first transatlantic service since the Boeing 720Bs left the airline's fleet.

After World War Two, American, British and French airlines had operating rights along the air corridors from and to West Berlin. Monarch had been operating charter flights to the Mediterranean from Berlin for West Berlin tour operator Flug-Union Berlin, since the start of the 1981 summer season. In 1988, a joint venture between Air France (51 per cent share) and Lufthansa (49 per cent share) established an airline called Euroberlin France to fly domestic services within West Germany. The Berlin Agreement agreed by the four wartime allies prevented Lufthansa's aircraft being used by Euroberlin. Instead, the new airline chose Monarch to provide the aircraft and flight crew under a wet-lease agreement, with locally recruited cabin staff. Aircraft maintenance and servicing support was provided by Monarch's subsidiary company, Monarch Aircraft Engineering, with a base established at Berlin-Tegel Airport. All administrative functions were carried out by Air France staff based in Paris. Monarch initially assigned four Boeing 737-300s, including three newly acquired aircraft, to the operation, and began flying at the start of the 1988–89 winter season from Berlin-Tegel Airport to Frankfurt, Cologne, Munich and Stuttgart. Two additional routes from Berlin to Düsseldorf and Hamburg were added at the start of the 1989 summer timetable. During the winter season of 1990/91, Monarch had nine aircraft operating for Euroberlin. The venture was short-lived, however, due to the collapse of communism in East Germany and the restoration of German unity in October 1990. Euroberlin continued to operate, but by 1991 it was using Air France and Lufthansa flight numbers. Monarch's aircraft gradually returned to the UK between early 1992 and December 1994 when the partnership finally ended, with the remaining two Boeing 737-300s returning to Monarch Airlines.

In preparation for extending its long-haul operations, Monarch signed a deal with Airbus in 1988 to purchase four A300-600Rs. The aircraft would be the airline's first wide-body type. The Airbus A300 was the first twin-engine wide-body airliner and the first wide-body aircraft to be produced in Europe. Development of the project began in 1967 when aircraft manufacturers in West Germany, France and the UK signed a memorandum of understanding to collaborate on the development of a new large

Monarch Airlines began operating aircraft for Euroberlin at the beginning of the winter season 1988–89. Shown here is Boeing 737-300 G-DHSW. (Fireballoons, distributed under a Creative Commons CC BY-SA 3.0 Licence)

Boeing 737-300 G-MONH being operated by Monarch on behalf of Euroberlin. (Pedro Aragão, distributed under a Creative Commons CC BY-SA 3.0 Licence)

Monarch's first wide-body aircraft type was the Airbus A300-605R. Shown here is the first A300 to be acquired by Monarch, G-MONR. (Aero Icarus, distributed under a Creative Commons CC BY-SA 2.0 Licence)

airliner. The UK government withdrew from the collaboration in April 1969, leaving West Germany and France to reach an agreement and formally create Airbus Industrie in December 1970, in order for the project to develop to fruition. The first variant of the A300 (designated the A300B1) made its maiden flight on 28 October 1972. The first production variant (A300B2) was larger than the original prototype, accommodating between 281 and 345 passengers and with a range of up to 1,850nm. Monarch ordered the upgraded A300-600 variant, which made its first flight in July 1983. It incorporated a redesigned wing, significant use of composite materials to reduce the overall weight of the aircraft and a two-crew cockpit with digital avionics and flight management systems and electronic instrument displays. With nine-abreast seating, the A300-600 was configured for Monarch to accommodate up to 361 passengers in a single-class configuration and to operate a range of up to 4,000nm.

In January 1989, Cosmos Tours (UK) Ltd, the parent company of Monarch Airlines, changed its status to a public limited company and was incorporated under the name of Monarch Holdings plc. Initially comprising Monarch Airlines Ltd, Monarch Aircraft Engineering Ltd and Cosmos Holidays, Monarch Holdings went on to own a number of subsidiaries, which included tour operators Distant Dreams, Archers, Direct Pullman Holidays and seat-only specialists Avro.

The first two A300s (G-MONR and G-MONS) were delivered in March/April 1990, followed by the remaining two in April/May 1991. Monarch was now able to use an aircraft with larger capacity from

Airbus A300-605R G-MONS at Manchester Airport. (Ken Fielding, distributed under a Creative Commons CC BY-SA 3.0 Licence)

Luton, Gatwick and Manchester for its most popular Mediterranean destinations and at peak times during the summer months and to ski resorts during the winter season. The A300 was also deployed on long-haul tour flights to an increasing range of destinations including the Bahamas, Brazil, Kenya, Malaysia, Mexico, Thailand, Southwest India, and to Florida, Boston and New York in the US.

After 22 years of the airline's administration and operations being based at Luton Airport, Monarch opened new, purpose-built headquarters at Luton in 1990, which contained many of the administrative and operational services required to run the airline as well as training facilities including the airline's £6 million Boeing 757 simulator.

During the early 1990s, Monarch operated several Boeing 767-300ERs on transatlantic flights for Alitalia Team, a subsidiary of Alitalia. The flights were operated under Monarch's air operator certificate until the Italian airline had obtained its own ETOPS certification.

In 1993, Monarch invested in more Airbus aircraft, introducing the A320-200 into the fleet to gradually replace the remaining Boeing 737-300s. The A320 was the first of the single aisle A320 family aircraft produced by Airbus, the programme being launched initially in 1984 as competition for the Boeing 737. It was the first civil airliner to include a digital fly-by-wire control system, which enabled Airbus to introduce a side-stick controller rather than the traditional yoke control column still found today in Boeing aircraft. In choosing the Airbus A320, Monarch was particularly impressed by its fuel efficiency and low operating costs. The aircraft's primary structures are built from various composite materials including carbon fibre and glass fibre-reinforced plastics to reduce the weight, and winglets, in the form of wingtip fences, improve the aerodynamic efficiency of the wings, consequently reducing fuel consumption. The A320 is also powered using efficient new generation turbofan engines (either the CFM International CFM56 or International Aero Engines (IAE) V2500s). Monarch's A320 cabins were fitted with a high density, one-class seating configuration and could accommodate up to 180 passengers. The first A320 (G-MONY) was delivered in January 1993 and the type remained a key component of the Monarch fleet until the demise of the airline in 2017.

In April 1993, Monarch celebrated 25 years of operations. The airline was now carrying in excess of three million passengers annually. With passenger demand increasing, Monarch introduced a frequent traveller incentive programme in September 1995 called Crown Advantage. Once a specific number of points had been accumulated from each flight, they could be redeemed for a larger free baggage allowance, access to executive airport lounges or discounted car parking at airports.

The second Airbus aircraft type to be operated by Monarch was the A320-200. G-OZBA was delivered to Monarch in March 1994. (Ken Fielding, distributed under a Creative Commons CC BY-SA 3.0 Licence)

Airbus A320-200 G-MPCD was delivered to Monarch in March 1994. (Aero Icarus, distributed under a Creative Commons CC BY-SA 2.0 Licence)

The largest member of the A320 family is the A321. G-OZBC, the first A321-231 acquired by Monarch, was delivered in April 1997. (Ken Fielding, distributed under a Creative Commons CC BY-SA 3.0 Licence)

Airbus A321-231 G-MARA seen here at Manchester in August 1999. G-MARA remained part of the Monarch fleet through to administration in October 2017. (Ken Fielding, distributed under a Creative Commons CC BY-SA 3.0 Licence)

Monarch Aircraft Engineering opened a second maintenance base at Manchester Airport in 1996, which included a dual bay hangar with sufficient space to handle both a narrow-body and a wide-body aircraft at the same time.

Another member of the Airbus A320 family joined Monarch in April 1997 when the airline acquired its first A321-200 (G-OZBC). This coincided with the last Boeing 737-300 leaving the fleet in May 1997. Several more A321s were delivered before the start of the 1999 summer programme, based at Birmingham and operating inclusive tour services. The A321 is the largest member of the A320 family, with the fuselage 22ft 9in longer than the A320 to give a maximum passenger capacity of 220.

In order to support its long-haul services, Monarch leased a McDonnell Douglas DC-10-30 (G-DMCA) from Chemco International Leasing in March 1996 and, the following year, took further steps to increase the number of wide-body aircraft in the fleet by placing an order for two Airbus A330-200s. The aircraft were due to be delivered early in 1998 in time for the summer season but, due to delays with delivery, the airline was forced to lease two McDonnell Douglas MD-11s from World Airways, with one aircraft (N273WA) operating between May and August 1998 and the other (N277WA) from August to November 1998, plus a Lockheed L1011-1 Tristar (TF-ABU) from Norske Finance Nederland for six months during the 1998 summer season.

McDonnell Douglas DC-10-30 G-DMCA was leased by Monarch in March 1996 to provide additional capacity on its long-haul services. (Pedro Aragão, distributed under a Creative Commons CC BY-SA 3.0 Licence)

Due to the delays in the delivery of several Airbus A330-200s, Monarch leased two McDonnell Douglas MD-11s to support its long-haul services. Shown here is N273WA at Zurich Airport in July 1998. (PropFreak)

McDonnell Douglas MD-11 N277WA was leased between August and November 1998. She is shown at Manchester in September 1998. (Ken Fielding, distributed under a Creative Commons CC BY-SA 3.0 Licence)

The Airbus A330s were eventually delivered to Monarch in March/April 1999. For the first time in Monarch's history, the aircraft were operated in a two-class configuration: Premium Cabin and Economy. Premium Cabin seats were available for a £30 supplement and provided 40 per cent extra legroom and more comfortable seating. Passengers opting for a Premium Cabin upgrade (the 'Monarch Plus' service) were also provided with a multi-channel entertainment system and complimentary headsets, a welcome drink and bar service, upgraded meal choices, increased baggage allowance and access to priority check-in, baggage handling and boarding at most airports. For the 1999 summer season, the A330s were used on non-stop, long-haul services from Gatwick and Manchester to destinations including Orlando, Las Vegas, Jamaica, Cuba and the Dominican Republic.

Lockheed L1011-1 Tristar TF-ABU was leased by Monarch for the 1998 summer season. (Aero Icarus, distributed under a Creative Commons CC BY-SA 2.0 Licence)

Crown Service

W I N T E R

97·98

T I M E T A B L E

MENORCA

MALLORCA

ALICANTE

MALAGA

GIBRALTAR

TENERIFE

Monarch
Airlines

Above: The first of two Airbus A330-220s, G-SMAN, was delivered to Monarch in March 1999. It is seen here at Manchester in April 1999. (Ken Fielding, distributed under a Creative Commons CC BY-SA 3.0 Licence)

Right: The cover of the winter 1997-98 Monarch Crown Service timetable, operating from Luton Airport. (Author's Collection)

Below: Airbus A330-200 G-EOMA, the second A330 to be acquired by Monarch. (Ken Fielding, distributed under a Creative Commons CC BY-SA 3.0 Licence)

Boeing 707-355C G-AXRS was operated by Monarch between April and December 1981. (Lewis Grant)

Boeing 737-200 G-GPAA at Faro in 1985. (Pedro Aragão, distributed under a Creative Commons CC BY-SA 3.0 Licence)

Boeing 737-200 G-BJSO taxiing at Faro, 1982. (Pedro Aragão, distributed under a Creative Commons CC BY-SA 3.0 Licence)

Right: Boeing 757-200 G-DAJB on stand at Zurich Airport in March 1995. (Aero Icarus, distributed under a Creative Commons CC BY-SA 2.0 Licence)

Below: Boeing 757-200 G-DRJC operated for Monarch between May 1987 and March 1993. (Pedro Aragão, distributed under a Creative Commons CC BY-SA 3.0 Licence)

Push-back of Monarch's Boeing 757-200 G-MCKE at Zurich in April 1995. (Aero Icarus, distributed under a Creative Commons CC BY-SA 2.0 Licence)

Boeing 757-200 G-MONJ at Alicante Airport, May 2004. (Hullie)

Boeing 757-200 G-MONE in a special Renaissance Cruises livery at Faro, July 1996. (Pedro Aragão, distributed under a Creative Commons CC BY-SA 3.0 Licence)

Boeing 757-200 G-MONE painted in the Renaissance Cruises livery. (Pedro Aragão, distributed under a Creative Commons CC BY-SA 3.0 Licence)

Boeing 737-300 G-MONG at Faro in 1989. (Pedro Aragão, distributed under a Creative Commons CC BY-SA 3.0 Licence)

Boeing B737-300 G-BNXW joined the Monarch fleet in October 1987 but only remained with the carrier for one year. (Aero Icarus, distributed under a Creative Commons CC BY-SA 2.0 Licence)

Boeing 737-300 G-MONH operating for Euroberlin (FotoNoir, distributed under a Creative Commons CC BY-SA 2.0 Licence)

Airbus A300-605R G-MAJS landing at Faro in 1991. (Pedro Aragão, distributed under a Creative Commons CC BY-SA 3.0 Licence)

Airbus A320-200 G-OZBB at Manchester Airport in February 1998. (Ken Fielding, distributed under a Creative Commons CC BY-SA 3.0 Licence)

Airbus A320-200 G-MPCD at Manchester in March 2002. (Ken Fielding, distributed under a Creative Commons CC BY-SA 3.0 Licence)

Airbus A321-200 G-OJEG, Monarch's third A321, was delivered prior to the start of the 1999 summer season. (Ken Fielding, distributed under a Creative Commons CC BY-SA 3.0 Licence)

McDonnell Douglas DC-10-30 G-DMCA at Manchester Airport on September 1998. (Ken Fielding, distributed under a Creative Commons CC BY-SA 3.0 Licence)

McDonnell Douglas DC-10-30 G-DMCA departing from Faro Airport, 1996. (Pedro Aragão, distributed under a Creative Commons CC BY-SA 3.0 Licence)

McDonnell Douglas MD-11 N277WA at Manchester Airport in September 1998. (David Caldwell)

Chapter 4

Changing Focus, Changing Brand (2000–09)

At the beginning of the 21st century, Monarch, along with traditional scheduled carriers and other charter airlines, was facing fierce competition from rapidly expanding low-cost, no-frills airlines such as Ryanair and easyJet. Following the liberalisation and deregulation of the commercial aviation industry in Europe in 1992, the sharp distinction between scheduled operators and charter carriers was reduced. Restrictions on seat-only flights were removed, creating an environment for low-cost airlines to begin to thrive and expand.

Charter airlines, such as Monarch, had historically been operating under low-cost principles, achieving cost efficiencies by operating high-density seating configurations in aircraft, high utilisation of aircraft and aircrew, high load factors on flights and by flying mostly short to medium distance routes, often to secondary airports. The operating costs of charter airlines were approximately 50 per cent of those of Europe's full service, scheduled airlines. The low-cost, no-frills airlines were essentially combining the low costs and fares associated with charter airlines with the convenience and frequency of flights associated with scheduled carriers, without the comfort and customer service.

The development of low-cost, no-frills airlines in Europe is largely associated with the emergence of Ryanair and easyJet. Ryanair was the first low-cost airline in Europe, which restructured its operations in 1991 and adopted a no-frills model. EasyJet was established in 1995 when it began flying services from Luton to Glasgow and Edinburgh. International services followed in 1997. Both airlines offered scheduled, seat-only services, as they continue to do today.

The competition faced by charter airlines from low-cost, no-frills carriers was focused on the destination. Low-cost carriers offered a more diverse range of destinations from a broader range of airports in the UK. Also flights were offered at a greater frequency than those available from charter carriers, either as part of an inclusive tour holiday or when sold as seat-only on a charter flight. This provided customers with greater flexibility and allowed them to create their own holidays rather than depend on package tour companies. Data from the Civil Aviation Authority (CAA) shows that charter traffic declined between 2000 and 2006, while scheduled flights increased significantly. For example, the number of passengers on charter flights from the UK to Malaga peaked at 2.4 million in 2000, declining to 900,000 in 2006. Conversely, the number of passengers on scheduled flights increased four-fold over the same time period, from 1 million to four million passengers, mainly due to low-cost carriers.

Charter airlines responded in different, mostly negative ways to the competition from low-cost carriers. By contrast, Monarch responded very positively, undergoing a significant amount of transformation. The airline had been operating some scheduled services since 1986 though its Crown Service brand. During 2000 it was operating scheduled services from Luton to Alicante, Faro, Gibraltar, Malaga, Menorca and Tenerife, and from Manchester to Alicante, Faro and Malaga. However, in 2000, less than 10 per cent of its passengers were carried by scheduled flights, with the majority still being transported on charter flights. The plan was to expand and increase the capacity on scheduled services. A first step was to introduce online booking in 2001, allowing customers to reserve flights without the need to book through a travel agent or use a call centre. This matched the easy access to online flight bookings characteristic of low-cost carriers.

In 2002, Monarch Crown Service was rebranded as Monarch Scheduled and simultaneously the airline introduced a new aircraft livery. The rebrand was a result of market research that revealed customers were confused by Monarch's scheduled flight package under the name of Crown Service. The word 'crown' no longer appeared to be associated with a specific premium service; passengers increasingly perceived it as an upgrade from the standard service. Under the rebranding, Monarch Scheduled continued to offer a similar full service product including free meals, complimentary drinks from the bar, hot towels, newspapers, in-flight entertainment and pre-booked seats free of charge, essentially a 'low-cost with frills' carrier.

The new aircraft livery was the airline's fourth and featured indigo and yellow flowing curves along the lower fuselage of the aircraft, which replaced the gold and black strips, and a white upper fuselage and vertical stabiliser. The crown logo on the vertical stabiliser remained but was redesigned.

Airbus A300-605R G-OJMR arriving at Palma Airport. (Ken Fielding, distributed under a Creative Commons CC BY-SA 3.0 Licence)

Airbus A330-200 G-EOMA painted in Monarch's fourth livery which was introduced in 2002. (Björn Strey, distributed under a Creative Commons CC BY-SA 2.0 Licence)

Boeing 757-200 G-DAJB on final approach into Manchester Airport. (Craig Sunter, distributed under a Creative Commons CC BY-SA 2.0 Licence)

About to depart Luton in February 2005 is Monarch's Airbus A320-200 G-OZBJ. (Arpingstone)

Airbus A321-231 G-OZBG taxiing at Geneva Airport, March 2007. (Aero Icarus, distributed under a Creative Commons CC BY-SA 2.0 Licence)

The initial expansion of services provided by Monarch Scheduled was focused away from Monarch's home base at Luton. During the late 1990s and early 2000s, low-cost, no-frills operators had expanded aggressively at both Luton and Stansted airports. Manchester already existed as a base for Monarch's scheduled services and, in 2003, a new scheduled base was opened at Gatwick Airport. Charter flights were already operating from Gatwick and the new scheduled routes included Alicante, Faro and Malaga. The early signs were very positive. Between 2000 and 2003, Manchester's scheduled programme saw a growth in summer season passenger numbers of 700 per cent compared with only 20 per cent at Luton. Passenger numbers at Gatwick on Monarch's scheduled summer programme were 75 per cent of those at Luton in just one season after it launched in April 2003. Building on the success at Manchester, Monarch added new scheduled services to Gibraltar, Tenerife and Barcelona in October 2003.

Despite a 74 per cent increase in the number of passengers carried by Monarch Scheduled in 2003, in an effort to reduce costs in 2004, the airline made a strategic decision to adopt a modified low-cost model for its scheduled services from July, making passengers pay for all food and drinks on scheduled flights. Trading performance had been challenging for the airline since 2001 as a consequence of the 9/11 terrorist attacks in the US and their impact on the aviation industry, together with the war in Iraq and the significant rise in global oil prices, which led to an increase in jet fuel costs. Despite these challenges, Monarch remained profitable.

In 2004, Monarch tried to improve the take-up of scheduled services from Luton by increasing the number of scheduled flights and, from the winter season of 2004/05, by introducing scheduled services to Lanzarote and Las Palmas. At Gatwick, Monarch Scheduled doubled the frequency of flights to Alicante and Malaga to two flights per day and retained the daily flight to Faro.

Monarch Scheduled opened its first overseas base at Malaga Airport in 2005, stationing there one Airbus A320, configured with 174 seats to provide additional leg room, together with a full crew. From November 2005, the A320 carried out daily flights from Malaga to Blackpool, three flights per week to Newquay and four flights per week to Aberdeen. The service between Malaga and Newquay came to an end in April 2006 due to the introduction of a departure levy at Newquay Airport, which made it more expensive to fly from Newquay than any other UK regional airport and consequently reduced the demand from overseas visitors. By the end of October 2006, the Blackpool service was discontinued due to low demand, and one year later the Malaga–Aberdeen route was withdrawn, leading to the closure of the Malaga base.

Back in the UK, Monarch Scheduled launched a new base at Birmingham Airport in April 2005, beginning with daily flights to Malaga and Tenerife. By September 2005, more than 160,000 passengers had travelled to and from Birmingham on Monarch Scheduled flights, leading to the company expanding its services from the airport the following summer with three new destinations: Murcia, Menorca and Palma. At Manchester, two new scheduled services to Madrid and Almeria were included in the 2005 summer season, which resulted in Monarch basing an additional Airbus A321 at the airport to operate the services. Monarch became Manchester Airport's second largest passenger airline in 2005, with 1.72 million passengers using the airport. In August 2005, more than 30,000 passengers were carried on the Manchester to Malaga scheduled service, the first time that the airline had achieved that number of monthly passengers on a single route. At Gatwick, new scheduled services to Granada and Lisbon were introduced in 2005.

By the end of 2005, Monarch was flying more than five million passengers for the second year in succession. Most of the growth in passenger numbers was for scheduled services, with Monarch Scheduled offering a network of 22 routes. In August 2005, Monarch Scheduled carried in excess of 300,000 passengers, almost 100,000 more than August 2004, with a load factor of 87 per cent. Scheduled services accounted for almost 50 per cent of Monarch's business in terms of passenger numbers. It was the first full year of ticketless operations for direct customers on scheduled services.

Fleet changes during the first five years of the decade included the retirement of the McDonnell Douglas DC-10 (G-DMCA) in October 2001, following more than five years of service for Monarch. The aircraft was broken up at Manchester Airport with the forward section of the fuselage, including the cockpit, donated to the Runway Visitor Park at the airport to be used as a learning resource, where it resides today. Two Airbus A320s were delivered to Monarch in April 2005, following the release of two aircraft in 2002 and 2004, leaving five A320s in the fleet at the end of 2005. The A321 fleet increased to seven with the delivery of six new aircraft between April 2000 and June 2004 and the withdrawal of two from service in 2000 and 2003. In April 2005, Monarch leased a Boeing 767-300ER (G-DIMB) for five years from MyTravel Airways to supplement the Airbus A330s on long-haul routes.

Above: In April 2005, Monarch leased Boeing 767-31 G-DIMB from MyTravel Airways. (Chris from Poznań, Poland, distributed under a Creative Commons CC BY-SA 2.0 Licence)

Left: Boeing 767-31 G-DIMB landing at Faro Airport, Portugal. (Pedro Aragão, distributed under a Creative Commons CC BY-SA 3.0 Licence)

Monarch's livery between 2002 and 2011 is clearly displayed on Airbus A320-200 G-MRJK. (Pedro Aragão, distributed under a Creative Commons CC BY-SA 3.0 Licence)

Airbus A320-200 G-OZBK, one of two A320s delivered to Monarch in April 2005. (Aero Icarus, distributed under a Creative Commons CC BY-SA 2.0 Licence)

Airbus A321 G-OZBF was delivered to Monarch in June 2002. (Ken Fielding, distributed under a Creative Commons CC BY-SA 3.0 Licence)

Airbus A321 G-OZBI in May 2008. (Andy Mitchell, distributed under a Creative Commons CC BY-SA 2.0 Licence)

In August 2006, Monarch announced the order of six Boeing 787-8 Dreamliners with an option for another four aircraft. The order was worth $916 million based on list prices at the time. The airliner featured advanced aerodynamics, including a variable-camber wing, an airframe constructed primarily of composite materials, which contributed to 50 per cent of the aircraft weight, extensive use of electrical systems and next-generation General Electric GEnx-1B or Rolls-Royce Trent 1000 high-bypass turbofan engines. All these features contributed to a 20–25 per cent reduction in fuel consumption, lower emissions and reduced noise levels during take-off and landing compared with similar aircraft, and this, together with the Dreamliner's size (able to accommodate up to 359 passengers in a single-class configuration), extended range (7,355nm) and faster cruise speeds made it highly suited to Monarch's business model, including both charter and scheduled operations. Although the airliner was yet to make its maiden flight at the time of the order, delivery was scheduled to start in 2010. Monarch intended to use the 787's long-range capabilities to open up new routes to destinations in North and South America, Asia and Africa. The plan was to initially replace the Airbus A300s in the fleet with the new 787s before moving towards an all-Boeing 787 wide-body fleet.

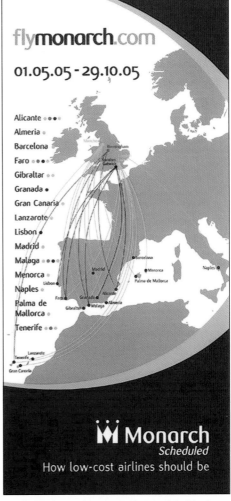

Destination map for Monarch Scheduled in the 2005 Summer Season (Author's Collection)

The first prototype Boeing 787 was rolled out of Boeing's Everett plant in July 2007 with a maiden flight scheduled for late August, but then came a series of problems. These included out-of-sequence production work, incomplete sub-assembly structures delivered to the final assembly line from suppliers, shortages of parts, supply chain issues, incomplete flight guidance software and a two-month strike by machinists. The maiden flight of the 787-8 didn't take place until December 2009, with a subsequent delay in the delivery of production aircraft to customers. For Monarch, it meant that the anticipated delivery of its first 787 was put back to 2013. The order was eventually cancelled in September 2011.

For the 2007 summer season, Monarch launched new scheduled services to Ibiza from Birmingham, Gatwick, Luton and Manchester in partnership with lifestyle-oriented music/club brand Hed Kandi. The partnership, named flyKandi, represented a strategic decision to target a new consumer base, essentially 18–30-year-old clubbers going to the island. One of Monarch's Boeing 757s was branded as a flyKandi aircraft and painted in a special livery. The partnership was renewed in 2008 and expanded to offer more party and clubbing destinations including Puerto Banús, Barcelona, Mallorca and Tenerife but it didn't continue into 2009.

Other new routes launched by Monarch Scheduled during 2007 included Luton to Almeria, Manchester to Jerez de la Frontera, Gatwick to Murcia and the airline's first scheduled flights to Larnaca (Cyprus) from Luton. However, scheduled services from Gatwick to Granada and Lisbon were withdrawn. From September 2007, Monarch aligned its low-cost business model closer to that of other low-cost, no-frills carriers by introducing a new baggage charge scheme for all hold baggage on scheduled flights.

Boeing 757-200 G-MONJ painted in a special flyKandi livery at Manchester in July 2008. (Chris Globe)

Boeing 757-200 (G-MOND) in a different version of the flyKandi livery at Faro Airport in July 2007. (Pedro Aragão, distributed under a Creative Commons CC BY-SA 3.0 Licence)

During 2007, Monarch transported more than six million passengers for the first time. Total passenger numbers had been growing annually by 6.2–8.7 per cent over the past four years. Almost 60 per cent of Monarch's passengers flew on scheduled services in 2007, compared to only 10 per cent in 2000.

Despite the major growth in scheduled services, the traditional charter business remained important to Monarch. In 2008, more than 16 million people in the UK were expected to take a package holiday that year, implying that a significant market still existed. Monarch was operating charter flights from 11 UK airports to around 30 destinations bordering the Mediterranean, North Africa, Florida and Mexico. Monarch considered itself to be the airline of choice for the UK's independent tour operators. However, rather surprisingly, Monarch changed its advertising slogan in 2008 from 'Let's make flying fun again' to 'The low fare airline that cares', essentially positioning itself as a low-cost airline but one that cared about quality and customer happiness. This was viewed in some quarters as a rebranding error, as Monarch was not a budget carrier or a premier airline.

In July 2008, Monarch provided one of its Airbus A321s for use in an ITV2 series called *CelebAir*, which involved various celebrities undertaking roles across the airline including cabin crew, check-in and ticket desk agents. Prior to starting the series, the celebrities completed Monarch's six-week training programme and were subsequently mentored and monitored by Monarch personnel. The celebrities were then placed on flights carrying fare-paying customers from Gatwick to a number of Monarch's scheduled destinations including Alicante, Malaga, Tenerife, Faro, Ibiza, Mahón and Larnaca.

Above: The advertising slogan introduced by Monarch in 2008, essentially positioning itself as a low-cost airline. (Monarch)

Right: Airbus A321-231 G-OZBI was used in the ITV2 series CelebAir. (DMK Photos, distributed under a Creative Commons CC BY 2.0 Licence)

Below: The CelebAir Airbus A321-231 G-OZBI departing from Faro, Portugal in July 2008. (Pedro Aragão, distributed under a Creative Commons CC BY-SA 3.0 Licence)

Airbus A321-231 G-OZBM landing at Manchester Airport. (Aero Icarus, distributed under a Creative Commons CC BY-SA 2.0 Licence)

Airbus A321-231 G-OZBR was acquired by Monarch in April 2008. It entered service almost immediately, still displaying a partial colourscheme from its previous operator, Spirit Airlines, but with Monarch titles and tail logo. (Alex Beltyukov, distributed under a Creative Commons CC BY-SA 3.0 Licence)

Airbus A321-231 G-OZBS taxiing at Gatwick Airport in July 2009. (Aero Icarus, distributed under a Creative Commons CC BY-SA 2.0 Licence)

Following the delivery of seven Airbus A321s between 2006 and 2008, Monarch's fleet increased to 33 aircraft as the airline aimed to expand scheduled services and provide additional capacity to its portfolio of charter customers. Several more A321s joined the fleet in February–March 2009. However, Monarch planned to operate only 32 aircraft during the summer of 2009, so, in November 2008, the carrier began a programme to reduce its fleet of seven Boeing 757s by retiring some of the oldest aircraft. Three 757s left the fleet in November 2008 (G-MONB, G-MONC and G-MONE), followed by a fourth (G-MOND) in January 2009. The sole Boeing 767 was returned to the lessor in March 2010.

After 41 years of continuous, mainly profitable activity, the financial year 2008/09, which ended on 31 October 2009, saw Monarch Holdings plc incurred a loss before tax of £30.4 million. This followed a profit of £6.7 million in 2007/2008. The substantial losses were largely attributed to high fuel costs subsequent to a doubling of the price of crude oil in the first half of the year, in addition to the challenge of passing these costs on to customers during a decline in market demand, with the UK in economic recession as a result of the global banking crisis. The cost of aviation fuel had been gradually increasing between July 2004 and July 2008 due to increases in the price of crude oil caused by a number of factors, including tensions in the Middle East, an increase in the demand for oil due to economic growth in Asia, especially China and India, and concerns around declining petroleum reserves and peak oil. In general, fuel costs for an airline such as Monarch were around 30 per cent of its total operational costs. However, in 2008 that proportion increased to 50 per cent.

Monarch Aircraft Engineering experienced a challenging period between 2000 and 2009. As with Monarch Airlines, the engineering subsidiary suffered a downturn in business following the events of 11 September 2001 in the US. At least one major third-party customer was lost due to the collapse of an airline. The merger of Thomas Cook with MyTravel, and that of First Choice with TUI in 2007 (Thomas Cook and First Choice being major customers of Monarch Aircraft Engineering), created some potential changes and possible growth opportunities for the maintenance business, but the demise of airlines and valued customers including FlyGlobespan, Zoom and Silverjet had a minimal impact on the business. A high degree of volatility characterised the aircraft maintenance environment throughout much of the ten-year period, although increasing market opportunities arose from a declining trend in maintenance capacity within the UK and Europe. In 2008/09, Monarch Aircraft Engineering experienced a significant increase in maintenance activity, although much of this was due to major 20-year maintenance checks on Monarch's Airbus A300 aircraft. The following year saw a decline in the business's third-party maintenance activity, which led to a number of redundancies in order to create a size of business consistent with a short–medium term decline in maintenance demand, with special consideration to the cyclical downturn in Monarch Airlines' scheduled aircraft maintenance.

Airbus A321-231 G-OZBT was acquired by Monarch in February 2009. (Ken Fielding, distributed under a Creative Commons CC BY-SA 3.0 Licence)

Airbus A321-231 G-OZBU departing from Faro Airport, Portugal. (Pedro Aragão, distributed under a Creative Commons CC BY-SA 3.0 Licence)

Boeing 757-200 G-MONJ at Geneva Airport. (Aero Icarus, distributed under a Creative Commons CC BY-SA 2.0 Licence)

Boeing 757-200 G-MONE about to depart from Runway 2 at Manchester Airport, July 2002. (Ken Fielding, distributed under a Creative Commons CC BY-SA 3.0 Licence)

Boeing 767-31 G-DIMB was leased by Monarch for five years, returning to the lessor in March 2010. (Pedro Aragão, distributed under a Creative Commons CC BY-SA 3.0 Licence)

Airbus A300-605R G-MONR touching down at Geneva. (Maarten Visser, distributed under a Creative Commons CC BY 2.0 Licence)

Airbus A300-605R G-OJMR at Hanover Airport, April 2009. (Björn Strey, distributed under a Creative Commons CC BY-SA 2.0 Licence)

Airbus A330-605R G-EOMA about to land at Faro Airport. (Pedro Aragão, distributed under a Creative Commons CC BY-SA 3.0 Licence)

Above: Airbus A330 G-SMAN was in service with Monarch between March 1999 and April 2015. (Aero Icarus, distributed under a Creative Commons CC BY-SA 2.0 Licence)

Right: The front fuselage section of McDonnell Douglas DC-10-30 G-DMCA preserved and on display at the Runway Visitor Park, Manchester Airport (Craig Sunter, distributed under a Creative Common CC BY 2.0 Licence)

Chapter 5

Financial Troubles and the End of Operations (2010–17)

Subsequent to the Monarch Group's first financial loss in its history in 2008/9, the company received a cash injection of £50 million from its major shareholder, the Mantegazza family. A detailed review of the Monarch Group's businesses, governance structure and senior management was undertaken in 2010, which resulted in extensive restructuring, aimed at focusing the Group's operations into six operating divisions: Scheduled Airline Activities, Charter Airline Activities, Airline Operations, Tour Operations, Aircraft Engineering and Retail and Online Activities. The expected outcome of the reorganisation was a more unified organisation with improved management and operational control of products and services within and between the divisions, leading to improved prospects for growth and financial performance.

The early part of 2010 was particularly challenging for Monarch, culminating in the Icelandic volcanic ash crisis in April, which led to the closure of the controlled airspace over many European countries for at least nine days and the cancellation of many flights. Nevertheless, Monarch introduced three new scheduled services in May to the Turkish destinations of Bodrum, Dalaman and Antalya. Customer demand was very strong during the summer, with Monarch Scheduled gaining record load factors during July and August, peaking at 94 per cent in August 2010, which was four per cent higher than the previous year. For most of the summer, Monarch operated with a fleet of 30 aircraft, following the return of the only Boeing 767 in the fleet to the lessor in March. At the end of the financial year, in October 2010, Monarch returned a profit of £1.5 million before tax, which was partly attributed to almost 25 per cent less expenditure on aviation fuel, a windfall of £4.4 million from the sale of several hangars at Luton Airport and a strong summer performance of both scheduled and charter operations.

In 2011, Monarch announced a strategic change in the focus of its business model from primarily a charter airline to predominantly a scheduled leisure operator, with the aim of operating around 80 per cent of its capacity on scheduled services in 2012. Associated with this change was an expansion strategy focused on increasing the scheduled network to new leisure destinations in Egypt, Turkey, Greece, Spain and Portugal. A modest number of new and additional scheduled flights was introduced in time for the 2011 summer season, including Luton to Corfu and services from Gatwick, Birmingham and Manchester to Bodrum. For the winter season, a new service from Gatwick to Barcelona was introduced and Monarch brought forward the launch of two new scheduled routes to Egypt, starting services to Sharm El-Sheikh from Gatwick and Manchester, ahead of its original planned summer 2012 launch.

Monarch's repositioning as a scheduled airline led to a relaunch of its brand in June 2011 using the advertising slogan, 'Fly your way. Every day'. The focus was to promote the services provided by the airline to allow customers greater flexibility to customise their own flight package, including booking allocated seats, extra leg-room, various in-flight meal options and airport lounge access. The rebranding included changes to the aircraft livery: the capital 'M' on the vertical stabiliser was painted in indigo and

Monarch.co.uk replaced *flymonarch.com* on the side of aircraft, together with the advertising slogan. As part of the brand relaunch, and in an attempt to increase its market attractiveness and be recognised by customers as a viable alternative to Ryanair and easyJet, Monarch removed the 3.5 per cent charge on all debit card bookings, at the same time introducing a single £10 flat rate fee on all credit card bookings. Monarch was the first airline to remove the debit card charge, considering it to be an upfront and transparent policy change that would differentiate it from other low-cost carriers.

Despite the restructuring, changes in business focus and rebranding, the Monarch Group reported a pre-tax loss of £70.2 million at the end of the financial year 2010/11. Positive financial performances by Tour Operations and Aircraft Engineering Services were offset by significant losses in Airline Operations. These losses largely resulted from the sale and lease-back arrangements of five Airbus A321 aircraft, capacity problems associated with the airline's ongoing migration to predominantly scheduled services, especially on West Europe routes, a stagnant economy in the UK and a sharp rise in the price of aviation fuel, which had increased the airline's fuel costs by £41 million compared with the previous year. In November 2011, the shareholders provided an additional £77 million of funding, bringing the total financial injection into the Group since October 2009 to £127 million. Along with the refinancing, the Monarch Group implemented a two-year turnaround plan, with a focus on restoring the Group to overall profitability by November 2013. This was to be achieved through a combination of cost savings and closer intra-division synergies, with clearly defined growth strategies for the airline, tour operations and engineering services.

Despite the financial difficulties, Monarch continued its expansion strategy in 2012, with the launch of 14 new scheduled services for the summer season, including Manchester to Dubrovnik, Milan, Venice and Verona; Luton and Birmingham to Rome; and flights from Birmingham and London Gatwick to Crete, Dubrovnik, Milan and Venice. In order to facilitate the expansion, two A320s (G-OZBW and G-OZBX) were added to the fleet in March 2012. These acquisitions represented the first stage of a medium-term (three- to five-year) plan to expand the fleet from 30 to around 40 aircraft in order to support the airline's objective of increasing annual passenger numbers from seven to 10 million.

Airbus A320-200 G-OZBK in a revised Monarch livery that was introduced in June 2011 together with the advertising slogan 'Fly your way. Every day' which was part of a brand relaunch (Jonathan Palombo, distributed under a Creative Commons CC BY 2.0 Licence)

Airbus A320-200 G-OZBW was one of two A320s acquired by Monarch in March 2012 (Nigel Richardson)

Airbus A320-200 G-OZBX at Birmingham Airport in February 2014. (Eric Salard, distributed under a Creative Commons CC BY-SA 2.0 Licence)

In August 2012, Monarch opened a new base at East Midlands Airport and introduced new routes to Malaga, Alicante, Palma, Faro and Lanzarote for the 2012/13 winter season, and added Ibiza to the summer 2013 destinations. The opportunity to open the new base arose from the departure of low-cost operator bmi baby from the East Midlands after its purchase by British Airways from Lufthansa. Monarch initially based two Airbus A321s at the airport to operate the new services.

By the end of the financial year in October 2012, there had been a 15.7 per cent increase (4.6 million to 5.3 million) in Monarch's scheduled passenger numbers and both tour operations and aircraft engineering reported profitable growth. These results, together with strong cost control, meant that the Group had made good progress in the first year of the turnaround plan, with a £31.6 million reduction in operating expenses and pre-tax losses reduced to £33.4 million. Further details of Monarch's revised plans for re-equipping its aircraft fleet were announced in November 2012. The airline proposed to order up to 45 aircraft to replace some of the existing aircraft and to contribute to an expansion of the fleet, with delivery up to 2021. Airbus, Boeing and Bombardier Aerospace were invited to submit strategic proposals for the supply of new aircraft, which would include both aircraft leasing and purchase options.

Leeds-Bradford Airport became Monarch's sixth base in March 2013, with two A320s based at the airport to operate 12 new scheduled services for the 2013 summer season to Antalya, Barcelona, Bodrum, Dalaman, Faro, Heraklion, Lanzarote, Larnaca, Majorca, Menorca, Rome and Tenerife. Monarch had operated a winter schedule 2012/13 from Leeds-Bradford to Munich and Grenoble, with the Munich service being retained for the summer of 2013. In order to support the development and growth of Monarch at Leeds-Bradford Airport through substantial marketing opportunities, the airline entered into a commercial partnership and sponsorship of Leeds United Football Club in December 2012.

The Monarch Group reduced operational expenditure by a further £20.3 million during 2012/13 and, with a 16 per cent increase in annual turnover, the Group returned to profitability with a pre-tax profit of £5.9 million. Monarch Airlines showed a significant improvement in its financial performance, attributed to a 15.1 per cent growth in scheduled passenger numbers (up to 6.1 million) and cost control measures. The growth in passenger numbers reflected the expansion from four to six bases, an increase in the number of destinations served by the airline, a growing public awareness of the Monarch brand and the introduction of an e-commerce strategy.

In November 2013, Monarch Aircraft Engineering opened a new £20m maintenance hangar at Birmingham Airport. The 110sq ft facility could accommodate two wide-body aircraft such as the Boeing 787 or up to ten narrow-body aircraft, and complemented Monarch's other engineering operations at Luton, Gatwick and Manchester airports. The facility allowed Monarch Aircraft Engineering to increase its proportion of third party (ie non-Monarch Airlines) maintenance work for airlines from the UK and Europe as well as supporting Monarch Airlines.

As part of the fleet expansion plan begun in 2012, Monarch took delivery of nine aircraft during 2013 – four A320s and five A321s – and retired two older A320s. However, at the end of the year, Monarch announced that it was considering proposals from Airbus, Boeing and Bombardier for new aircraft to be delivered by 2024. The aircraft under consideration included the Airbus A320neo and A321neo, the Boeing 737 MAX and the Bombardier CS-100 and CS-300. Monarch stated that the contract awarded to the successful tender was potentially worth $6bn and would deliver a young fleet of approximately 62 aircraft following the retirement of some existing aircraft. The outcome of the tender deliberations was announced at the Farnborough Airshow in July 2014. Boeing was selected as the preferred bidder and Monarch confirmed that it would be placing an order for 30 737 MAX 8s worth more than $3.1bn at 2014 list prices, including options for 15 additional aircraft. Monarch considered the 737 MAX to be the best fit for its scheduled airline business model as it offered high reliability, passenger comfort and cost efficiency, with a predicted eight per cent operating cost per seat advantage over the A320neo.

Monarch took delivery of four A320-200s during 2013, one of which was G-OZBY seen here landing at Manchester Airport in August 2014 (Nigel Richardson)

Airbus A320-200 G-ZBAH was delivered to Monarch in June 2013. (Nigel Richardson)

Airbus A321-231 G-ZBAD, one of five A321s acquired by Monarch during 2013. (Nigel Richardson)

Airbus A321-231 G-ZBAE about to depart Manchester Airport, September 2016. (Nigel Richardson)

Monarch placed an order for thirty Boeing 737-8 MAXs in October 2014. Here is an artist's impression of the 737-8 MAX in Monarch livery. (Boeing)

A concept image of a Boeing 737-8 MAX in Monarch livery. (Boeing)

The Boeing 737 MAX was launched in July 2011 and is the fourth generation of the 737. It succeeds the 737 Next Generation (NG) series and features airframe and aerodynamic modifications, including split-tip winglets, and is powered by CFM International LEAP-1B high by-pass turbofan engines. The 737 MAX 8 was the first variant of the 737 MAX to be developed and can carry up to 178 passengers in a single class seating configuration.

Although everything seemed positive and exciting for Monarch, in July 2014 the Group undertook a significant restructure, including three new appointments to fill the positions of Chair, Chief Executive Officer and Chief Financial Officer. One month after their appointment, the new board announced a strategic review of the Group. All elements of the business were to be considered including operations, ownership and financing, suggesting all was not well. Monarch stated that the objective of the review was to 'determine the optimum structure to realise the significant opportunity to build on the respected Monarch brand and distinctive offer to its customers in the budget airline market'. At the time it was rumoured that a number of private equity investors were considering inputting cash into the company and that one outcome may be new shareholders and a new owner. Monarch required £60m to help fund the purchase of the 737 Max 8s as part of the fleet renewal plan. A number of key developments began to emerge from the review in September 2014.

The Monarch Group, including the airline, tour operations and aircraft engineering, accepted a bid from private investment company Greybull Capital to acquire the Group from its existing shareholders, principally the Mantegazza family. The sale was completed in late October 2014. Greybull acquired 90 per cent ownership in Monarch, the remaining 10 per cent being held by the Group's pension protection fund. As part of the deal, Monarch secured £125m of new capital, with £75m reportedly provided by Greybull Capital and £50m from the Group's prior shareholders (the Mantegazza family) in order to facilitate the take-over transaction. The sale of the Group was completed just hours before Monarch's operating licence from the CAA was due to expire.

The strategic review confirmed a decision to complete Monarch's transition to an entirely scheduled low-cost carrier. All long-haul and charter operations were designated to end by April 2015. The focus of operations from May 2015 was on short-haul routes to leisure destinations in the southern Mediterranean, Canary Islands and Turkey, together with flights to European cities and skiing destinations. The aim was to fly more frequently to fewer destinations, increasing aircraft utilisation, productivity and profitability. The flight requirements of Monarch's tour operations' division, including Cosmos Holidays and Avro, were to be provided through Monarch's scheduled operations and third-party carriers. One consequence of the route network review and subsequent changes to the flying schedule was the end of operations and closure of the base at East Midlands Airport by the end of April 2015.

A further consequence of the review was a reduction in the fleet size from 42 to 34 aircraft in 2014, as well as a renegotiation of the leases on ten aircraft, with the possibility of the return of some of these aircraft to the lessors. The view was that overcapacity had been a major problem. Monarch had grown too fast and ended up with too many aircraft and too few passengers, a problem exacerbated by the expansion of competitors Ryanair and easyJet and the entry of new rivals, such as Norwegian Airlines, which had caused a fall in seat prices. Unable to charge higher fares in order to generate sufficient revenue to offset high costs without the risk of losing market share, Monarch was faced with significant losses. Under-utilisation of aircraft may also have been a problem. Due to the nature of Monarch's operational focus on leisure destinations, there would have been greater demand during the summer months than in the winter. With a predominantly leased fleet, the cost of lease payments is incurred throughout the year whether or not the aircraft fly and generate revenue. Nonetheless, the purchase of 30 737 MAX 8s was supported by the new owners and the order was finalised in October 2014, with deliveries scheduled to begin in early–mid 2018. It was estimated that the acquisition of the 737 MAX 8s would lead to fuel and maintenance savings of £2–3m annually per aircraft.

The review also impacted Monarch's workforce, resulting in up to 700 staff redundancies of which two-thirds were voluntary. Pilots, cabin crew and engineering staff also agreed to pay cuts of up to 30 per cent and changes to working conditions.

Monarch's Annual Report and Financial Statement for the financial year ending 31 October 2014 confirmed the Group's financial problems and the reasons for the decisions taken following the strategic review. A loss before tax of £57.3m was reported. The total passenger numbers carried by the airline had increased slightly by 0.4 per cent but an increase in capacity, due to three more aircraft being operated, had resulted in a 6.5 per cent reduction in the load factor. Due to weak customer demand and an overall increase in market capacity, the price per seat had decreased by almost seven per cent, with the net result being a significant reduction in revenue and a reported loss of £206.2m. Fleet changes during the financial year included the acquisition of six A321s and two A320s and the withdrawal of two A320s and the last three A300s.

Above: Airbus A320-200 G-ZBAP, one of two A320s acquired by Monarch during 2014. (Nigel Richardson)

Left: Airbus A320-200 G-ZBAR landing at Manchester Airport in March 2017. (Riik@mctr, distributed under a Creative Commons CC BY-SA 2.0 Licence)

Airbus A321-231 G-ZBAI was the first of six A321s delivered to Monarch during 2014. (Nigel Richardson)

Airbus A321-231 G-ZBAL departing from Manchester, August 2014. (Nigel Richardson)

Boeing 757-200 G-MONK was one of the final three Boeing 757s to operate for Monarch before withdrawal in November 2014. (Nigel Richardson)

Boeing 757-200 G-DAJB taxies in at Manchester in July 2014. The aircraft was withdrawn from service in November 2014. (Nigel Richardson)

Downsizing of the fleet began in earnest in November–December 2014 with the departure of the three remaining Boeing 757s, one A320 and two A321s. Although two A320s were delivered in 2015, three A320s were retired and the two A330s were withdrawn from service, with wide-body aircraft no longer required following the withdrawal of long-haul services. The review of Monarch's operations led to a number of routes being dropped from all of its bases except Leeds-Bradford, including six from Manchester and three each from Gatwick, Birmingham and Luton. Another eight routes ended following the closure of the base at East Midlands Airport. However, new scheduled routes to Preveza, Rhodes and Zakynthos in Greece were included for the 2015 summer season, although these had previously been part of Monarch's charter services. For Monarch's newest base, Leeds-Bradford Airport, there were two new routes to Alicante and Naples. The airline was flying to 33 destinations in 12 countries, with more than 50 per cent of all flights to Spain, 11.5 per cent to Portugal and 9.6 per cent to Turkey.

Following the reduction in operations and the end of charter flying from the start of the summer season, Monarch carried 5.7 million passengers during 2015 (5.98 million during the 2014/15 financial year), a decline of 18.6 per cent compared with the previous year. Flight bookings, especially during the summer period, had suffered from the impact of the beach terrorist attack in Tunisia in June 2015, which effectively closed the country as a holiday destination for British tourists, as well as the Greek Eurozone crisis (leading to a 50 per cent decline in bookings for July and August), and the migrant crisis in the eastern Mediterranean. However, bookings to western Mediterranean destinations and the Canary Islands were above expected levels, partly due to the problems in other destinations but also because of a beneficial Euro exchange rate. At the end of the 2014/15 financial year, the Monarch Group reported a pre-tax profit of £19.2 million, with the airline making a pre-tax profit of £26.9 million, the second net profit since 2008. Restructuring and the reduction in the number of aircraft used had contributed to a significant decrease in the airline's operating costs.

Expansion of the route network for the 2015/16 winter season included ski services from Gatwick to Innsbruck, Geneva and Salzburg, and from Manchester to Geneva and Lyon. New flights were arranged to popular winter destinations in Spain, including Alicante, Majorca, Menorca, Lanzarote, Gran Canaria and Madeira, and two new routes were launched to Tel Aviv and Ovda in Israel. This was succeeded by five new routes to Lisbon, Madrid and Tel Aviv in summer 2016, plus six additional routes to destinations already served by Monarch (Almeria, Funchal, Gibraltar, Gran Canaria and Malaga). Eight routes were withdrawn, resulting in the end of scheduled services to Agadir, Bodrum, Enfidha and Zakynthos. The only change to the aircraft fleet during 2016 was the addition of one A320 and the wet-lease of an A320 (YL-LCP) from SmartLynx Airlines.

In September 2016, negative speculation concerning Monarch's finances suggested that the company was in trouble financially and on the verge of bankruptcy. Monarch strongly denied the rumours, although sources hinted that it was in discussion with various parties, including the Chinese HNA Group, about a potential takeover. The CAA became aware of Monarch's financial problems during the annual renewal process for its Air Travel Organiser's Licence (ATOL), being concerned that the airline would be unable to meet its renewal requirements at the end of the month. (The CAA will not issue ATOL licences where an airline may be experiencing significant financial difficulties, as it demonstrates a significant risk of insolvency.) As a contingency, the CAA made the necessary preparations for a 'shadow airline' to be established; spare aircraft were commandeered from other airlines in order to undertake the potential repatriation of approximately 180,000 British citizens who may be left stranded abroad should Monarch go into administration. The cost of these arrangements was reported to be £25.6 million. On 30 September, following discussions with the airline, the CAA granted Monarch a 12-day extension to its ATOL licence after the majority shareholder, Greybull Capital, confirmed that it would be putting

Airbus A320-200 G-ZBAT, the penultimate A320 to be delivered to Monarch Airlines. (Nigel Richardson)

Airbus A320-200 G-ZBAU was the last A320 to be acquired by Monarch in April 2016. It is seen here landing at Barcelona Airport in July 2016. (James Abbott, distributed under a Creative Commons CC BY 2.0 Licence)

Airbus A320-200 YL-LCP was wet-leased from SmartLynx by Monarch for the 2016 and 2017 summer season. (Riik@mctr, distributed under a Creative Commons CC BY-SA 2.0 Licence)

additional funds into the company. On 12 October 2016, Monarch successfully retained its ATOL licence after an £165 million investment from Greybull. It was thought that the financial package involved an agreement between Greybull Capital and Boeing over the terms of Monarch's order for 30 (plus 15 options) 737 MAX 8 aircraft, whereby all or part of the purchase agreement was restructured into a sale and leaseback arrangement, which would free up funds for a cash injection into the airline. However, one year later, it was reported that Boeing had provided £100 million of the £165 investment through payments to Monarch's holding company, Petrol Jersey Ltd, over a six-month period from October 2016, to ensure that the airline remained operational and to protect its 737 MAX order.

Monarch's financial statement for 2015/16 was not released until August 2017. It revealed the serious financial predicament of the Group during 2016. The Group loss before tax was £297.9 million, with the airline reporting a loss of £291.1 million for the year up to the end of October 2016. The airline had faced a number of challenges during the year that had impacted on its financial performance and resulted in an almost 15 per cent fall in revenue. There had been a 50–60 per cent downturn in bookings for flights to and from Turkey owing to terrorist incidents, together with a UK government ban on all direct flights to Tunisia from July 2015 and to Sharm El-Sheikh in Egypt from November 2015 following terrorist attacks. The Brexit referendum in June 2016 led to a decline in bookings in the lead-up to and immediately after the result for Britain to leave the EU. This was compounded by a 20 per cent fall in the value of the pound sterling against the US dollar and the euro. Monarch's outgoings, especially for fuel and aircraft leases, were paid in US dollars and euros, while most of the revenue income was in pounds sterling. Passenger numbers declined by 6.8 per cent to 5.57 million during the 2015/16 financial year (5.43 million during 2016), together with a 5.3 per cent decrease in the load factor. Other factors that contributed to the major losses included intense competition from other low-cost airlines and a depressed economy. The Tour Operations' division suffered from similar issues to those experienced by the airline during 2015/16, which led to a 36.9 per cent decrease in revenue and a £5.3 million loss before tax. However, Monarch Aircraft Engineering reported a pre-tax profit of £10.4 million.

The Monarch Group responded in a number of ways to the challenging environment in which it was operating. The route network continued to be developed, with the opening of new routes to Turin, Kittilä, Innsbruck and Lisbon for the 2016/17 winter season, followed by new scheduled services to Porto, Stockholm and Zagreb (a total of 13 new routes) from April/May 2017. In addition, a decision was taken for the Tour Operations' division to only sell holiday packages that made sole use of Monarch Airline's flights rather than flights provided by third-party operators. There was significant investment in marketing initiatives, including the use of social media and a television advertising campaign, to increase public awareness of the Monarch brand.

Competition from other low-cost carriers on Monarch's routes intensified in 2017, with even more capacity redeployed, partly as a consequence of the reduction in the number of flights to Turkey, Tunisia and Egypt, and air fares were cut as airlines battled to grow their market share. The Tour Operations' division also faced increased competition from larger rivals, such as Thomas Cook Holidays and TUI, as well as online travel agents. While flight-only bookings and holiday bookings increased, falling ticket prices and the devaluation of the pound led to further losses for the airline, although its cash position was reportedly healthier than it had been in recent years. In April 2017, Monarch arranged an independent review of the business by an aviation consultancy. The review, produced in late August, forecast that the airline would face substantial losses in the 2017/18 financial year and that it would require significant new investment or need to be sold to pay its debts. The review also proposed that while a potential change to a long-haul business model could prove profitable, options to improve the short-haul network were limited.

At the end of September 2017, Monarch, once again, faced the renewal of its ATOL licence. Monarch's directors had already made the CAA aware of their concerns about the airline's medium- and long-term future, due to the competitive market and the difficult trading conditions. They were considering a number of options, including the sale of some of the Group's assets or subsidiary companies, and were also contemplating repositioning as a long-haul airline as recommended by the independent review. Unions representing the airline's workforce requested financial help from the UK government, but a bridging loan to allow the airline to restructure its operations wasn't offered. There had been an expression of interest in the purchase of the business as a going concern but, following talks, the potential buyer decided not to proceed. Further investment from the company's major shareholders or from other sources was not forthcoming.

Monarch failed to meet the financial standards required to renew its ATOL licence, despite being granted a 24-hour extension by the CAA from midnight on the 30 September 2017 for emergency talks with the regulator. Following the licence extension, Monarch tripled its fares to deter any new bookings and reduce further exposure to claims should it collapse. With only 40 minutes remaining until midnight on 1 October and expiry of the ATOL licence, Monarch cancelled two flights to Ibiza from London Gatwick and Birmingham at the boarding stage. At 03.19am on 2 October, the airline's final service flight from Tel Aviv landed at Manchester Airport. At 4.00am, the CAA confirmed that the Monarch Airlines Group, except for Monarch Aircraft Engineering Ltd, had ceased operations with immediate effect and entered into administration. Monarch collapsed with debts of £630m, of which £466m was unsecured. At the time, it was the UK's largest ever airline to cease operations. Some 100,000 customers were stranded overseas, unaware that their return flights to the UK no longer existed. About 50 per cent were ATOL-protected, providing them with the assurance of being flown back at no extra charge.

Aware of Monarch's financial difficulties, the CAA had spent several weeks preparing to implement its pre-existing contingency plans in case the airline collapsed. Following administration, the UK government instructed the CAA to bring back to the UK all of Monarch's customers, whether or not they were ATOL-protected. This led to the UK's largest peacetime repatriation effort. The CAA commandeered a fleet of more than 60 aircraft from 24 airlines. A wide range of aircraft were used, including Airbus A320s, A321s, A330s and A340s and Boeing 737s, 747s, 757s, 767s and 777s. Around 85,000 passengers were flown back to the UK over a period of two weeks, from 33 airports in 14 countries. In total, 98 per cent of the passengers arrived back in the UK on the same day that they had originally booked, mostly from Spain and Portugal. Those passengers that did not use the repatriation flights had made alternative travel arrangements. The cost of the repatriation operation was £60 million.

At the time of administration, Monarch had a fleet of nine A320-200s, 25 A321-300s and a single Boeing 737-800 (G-ZBAV), which had been leased from Pegasus Airlines in preparation for the arrival of the first 737 MAX 8s. All the A320 and A321 aircraft were on lease arrangements. The company employed approximately 1,900 staff.

The demise of Monarch could be attributed to a combination of several external factors:

- The airline's decision to move away from long-haul flights and become a low-cost carrier, focusing on short-haul routes in a market with intense competition from Ryanair, easyJet, WizzAir and Norwegian Air Shuttle. As a new entrant into an already very competitive market, Monarch didn't differentiate itself sufficiently to be a credible competitor. Over-capacity on routes to southern Europe led to low fares as the carriers competed for a substantial market share, which eventually impacted revenue.
- The depreciation of the pound sterling against the US dollar and the euro following the EU referendum, which increased the airline's operating costs, especially the cost of aviation fuel. Aircraft leases, fuel, airport landing fees and ground-handling charges were paid in dollars and euros, while nearly all of Monarch's revenue was in sterling. The decline in the value of the pound diminished any revenue benefit but led to big increases in costs.
- Terrorist activity in Tunisia, Sharm El-Sheikh and Turkey in 2015 resulted in the airline ceasing to operate to and from Tunisia and Sharm El-Sheikh and led to a significant decline in demand for Turkish destinations, with significant repercussions on Monarch's income. Furthermore, redeployment of its Egypt, Tunisia and Turkey capacity to Spain and Portugal further intensified the competition with other low-cost carriers.

Monarch Aircraft Engineering Ltd, based at Luton, continued to operate after the collapse of the Monarch Group and was taken over by Greybull Capital in October 2018. However, the company began to lose customers and inherited significant debts and claims following the insolvency of Monarch Airlines. It entered administration at the beginning of January 2019, leading to the loss of 408 jobs.

Boeing 737-800 G-ZBAV was leased by Monarch in May 2017 in preparation for the arrival of the first Boeing 737-8 MAXs. (Alec Wilson, distributed under a Creative Commons CC BY-SA 2.0 Licence)

Airbus A300-605R G-MONS on final approach to Gatwick Airport, September 2013. (aeroprints.com, distributed under a Creative Commons CC BY-SA 3.0 Licence)

Airbus A300-650R G-OJMR was the last A300 to be withdrawn from the Monarch fleet in April 2014. (Nigel Richardson)

Above: Both of Monarch's A330s were withdrawn from service in April 2015. A330-200 G-SMAN is seen here at Manchester in July 2014. (Nigel Richardson)

Right: Airbus A330-200 G-EOMA landing at Hannover Airport, March 2012. (Björn Strey, distributed under a Creative Commons CC BY-SA 2.0 Licence)

Airbus A320-200 G-ZBAS taxiing to the terminal buildings at Manchester. (Nigel Richardson)

Airbus A320-200 G-OZBB with a special logo to celebrate the wedding of Prince William and Kate Middleton in April 2011. (Craig Sunter, distributed under a Creative Commons CC BY 2.0 Licence)

Airbus A321-231 G-MARA was one of the longest operating aircraft for Monarch, from March 1999 to October 2017. (Nigel Richardson)

Airbus A321-231 G-ZBAK at Manchester Airport in August 2014. (Nigel Richardson)

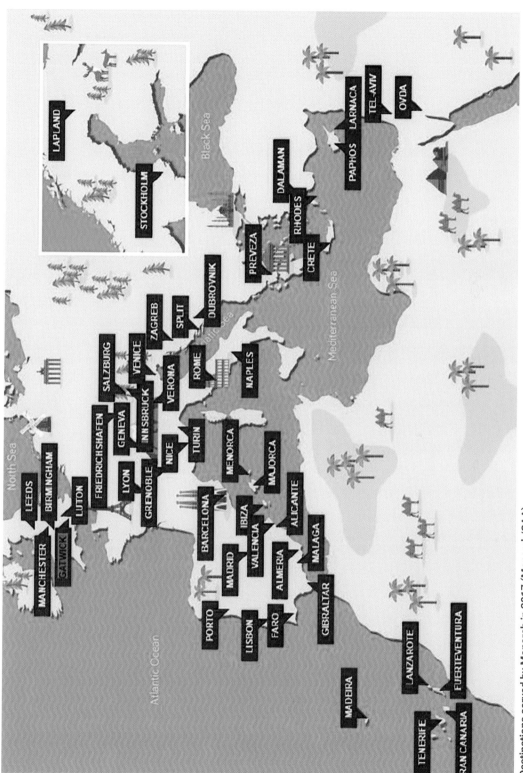

Destinations served by Monarch in 2017 (Monarch/CAA)

Above: Airbus A321-231 G-ZBAO was the last A321 acquired by Monarch, in May 2014. (Nigel Richardson)

Left: Messages sent out to Monarch customers, both in the UK and abroad, by the CAA via Twitter on the day the airline went into administration. (CAA)

Incidents and Accidents

Sources
Aero Inside (aeroinside.com)
Air Accident Investigation Branch (www.gov.uk/aaib-reports)
Air Accident Investigation Unit Ireland (www.aaiu.ie)
Aviation Safety Network (aviation-safety.net)
Comisión de Investigación de Accidentes e Incidentes de Aviación Civil
The Aviation Herald (https://avherald.com/)

January 1985
A Boeing 757-200 operating flight MON390 from Tenerife to Luton experienced two mid-flight explosions causing the aircraft to lose electrical power and make an emergency landing in Portugal. The cause was lavatory liquid (Blue Loo) leaking on to damaged Kapton insulated wire leading to arcing, an explosion and fire.

25 November 1998
A Boeing 767-300 (G-DIMB) operating a flight from Las Vegas to Manchester Airport suffered major damage to a cabin floor beam and damage to the standby system power supply cable, causing electrical arcing. The damage was discovered during unloading at Manchester and was caused by the movement of two baggage containers during take-off and in flight.

22 January 2000
A Boeing 757-200 (G-MONE) operating a flight from Salzburg to London Gatwick experienced problems with the nose landing gear on approach to Gatwick. The aircraft was able to land safely; however, various mechanical components of the nose landing gear had failed due to metal fatigue.

22 May 2002
A Boeing 757-200 (G-MONC) operating from Luton to Gibraltar suffered structural damage to the forward fuselage in the area of the nose wheel during landing at Gibraltar Airport. The nose of the aircraft pitched down rapidly after the main wheel touchdown, causing the nose wheel to impact the runway. The cause was considered to be due to an incorrect landing technique involving the use of full nose-down elevator on landing.

17 March 2006
During the approach to Gibraltar Airport, the flight crew of Boeing 757-200 (G-MONE) from London Luton lost visual contact with the runway after passing the visual decision point. A go-around was performed. However, the crew did not follow the correct procedures for a missed approach. Air traffic control had to provide effective heading control to prevent the aircraft from hitting high ground.

21 May 2008
An Airbus A321-231 (G-OZBI) operating flight ZB3347 from Paphos to Birmingham had to return to Paphos just 15 minutes into the flight, when a cockpit warning light indicated that a cargo door was open. Subsequent inspection revealed that the cargo door was closed and the warning light was faulty.

9 June 2008
An Airbus A300-600 (G-MONS) operating flight ZB7908 from London Gatwick to Corfu suffered a burst tyre on landing and became stranded on the runway.

29 July 2008
During landing at Manchester Airport, an Airbus A321-231 (G-MARA), operating flight ZB661 from Malaga, flared early causing it to 'float' approximately 10 feet above the runway, before a nearly flat touchdown with the nose wheel first followed by a significant bounce. It was subsequently discovered that the heavy landing had caused damage to various mechanical components of the nose landing gear.

3 July 2009
An Airbus A320-231 (G-MPCD) operating flight ZB648 from Manchester to Larnaca had to divert to Munich due to smoke in the cabin. The aircraft landed safely.

3 August 2010
During the initial climb from Birmingham Airport, the left-hand engine of an Airbus A321-231 (G-MARA), operating flight ZB932 to Tenerife, emitted a loud bang, streaks of flames and black smoke. The engine was shut down and the aircraft returned safely to Birmingham. Subsequent inspection indicated an engine fire.

10 September 2010
An Airbus A321-231 (G-OZBS) operating flight ZB1607 from Zakynthos to Birmingham had to divert to Athens as the landing gear would not retract after departure from Zakynthos.

4 November 2010
An Airbus A300-600 (G-MONR) operating flight ZB4952 from Manchester to Sharm El-Sheikh (Egypt) suffered a crack in the windshield, about 80nm north of Split (Croatia), two hours into the flight. The aircraft descended to a lower altitude and returned safely to Manchester.

21 May 2011
An Airbus A321-231 (G-OZBS) operating flight ZB7526 from Dublin to Las Palmas was unable to accept the active runway 16 for departure due to performance limitations. During taxi to runway 28, the aircraft did not follow the taxi clearance correctly and proceeded to enter runway 16 and stop, but at the same time as a Ryanair 737-800 was accelerating for departure on the same runway. The Ryanair crew conducted a high-speed rejected take-off and stopped approximately 260m from the A321.

26 July 2011
During the initial climb out from Gatwick Airport, the angle of attack of Airbus A300-600 (G-MAJS), operating flight ZB1472 to Chania (Greece), increased above 7.5 degrees, the airspeed decreased and the stall-protection system activated twice. The flaps and slats had been retracted in error instead of the landing gear.

20 May 2012
The crew of an Airbus A320-200 (G-OZBX), operating flight ZB5479 from Milan Malpensa to Birmingham, had to initiate an emergency descent southwest of Lille, France, from FL380 to FL100 due to a loss of cabin pressure. The aircraft continued to Birmingham and landed safely. The lost cabin pressure was due to a technical issue with one of the aircraft's engines.

31 May 2012
An Airbus A321-231(G-OZBT), operating flight ZB532 from Manchester to Palma, Mallorca, was diverted to London Gatwick due to a smell of smoke in the cabin. After safely landing at Gatwick it was determined that the smell was due to the unruly behaviour of a passenger singeing the hair of a fellow passenger.

12 June 2012
A Boeing 757-200 (G-DAJB) operating flight ZB3789 from Chania, Greece, had to divert to Munich Airport when the crew reported smoke in the cockpit.

24 July 2012
The crew of a Boeing 737-400 (ON-AEX), operated by AirExplore on behalf of Monarch Airlines, on flight ZB958 from Birmingham to Palma, Mallorca, had to initiate an emergency descent north of Limoges, France, from FL350 to FL130 due to a loss of cabin pressure. The aircraft diverted to Limoges and landed safely.

21 September 2012
A Boeing 737-300 (LY-SKA), operated by charter Aurela on behalf of Monarch Airlines, on flight ZB467 from Nice to Birmingham, landed at Birmingham but overran the runway and the runway end safety area before coming to a stop on the airfield grassed area. No injuries were reported.

8 August 2013
The crew of an Airbus A300-600 (G-MAJS), operating flight ZB248 from London Gatwick to Sharm El-Sheikh (Egypt), had to shut down the left-hand engine as the aircraft descended to land, due to fuel no longer reaching the engine.

4 October 2013
The crew of an Airbus A320-200 (G-OZBB), operating flight ZB239 from Lanzarote to London Gatwick, had to perform a high-speed rejected take-off due to an engine failure.

7 June 2014
A Boeing 757-200 (G-DAJB), operating flight ZB279 from Barcelona to London Gatwick, was accelerating for take-off when the crew performed a high-speed rejected take-off due to an engine fault.

1 July 2015
An Airbus A321-231 (G-OZBI), operating flight ZB714 from London Gatwick to Larnaca, was intercepted by two Croatian Air Force MiG-21s at the Slovenia/Croatia border. The MiG-21s were dispatched by NATO headquarters to intercept and identify the aircraft after it failed to communicate with air-traffic control while flying over Slovenia. The aircraft was identified as a Monarch A321 and was accompanied to the Croatia/Bosnia-Herzegovina border.

27 August 2015

Cabin crew on an Airbus A321-231 (G-OZBI), operating flight ZB472 from Birmingham to Sharm El-Sheikh, had to extinguish a fire in the toilet while en route. A second fire started and was again extinguished by the cabin crew. The aircraft made a safe landing in Sharm El-Sheikh. Following investigation, a male passenger on the flight was found guilty of starting both fires.

18 October 2015

An Airbus A321-231, operating flight ZB654 from Manchester to Malaga, had to return to Manchester shortly after take-off when it was noticed that a loose part was hanging off the right-hand wing.

29 March 2016

An Airbus A321-231 (G-OZBH), operating flight ZB627 from Lanzarote to Manchester, had to make a low-speed rejected take-off due to an engine failure.

16 March 2017

An Airbus A321-231 (G-OZBU), operating flight ZB970 from Birmingham to Malaga, had to make a high-speed rejected take-off after an engine overheated during the take-off run.

21 July 2017

An Airbus A321-231 (G-OZBH), operating flight ZB942 from Birmingham to Menorca and fully established on the final stage of an instrument landing system (ILS) approach into Menorca had to carry out a go-around procedure after a private Aquila A 210 crossed beneath the A321. The private aircraft had been cleared by air traffic control to cross through the Menorca Terminal Control Area behind the Monarch A321, but had confused it with another aircraft, which was on approach ahead of the Monarch A321.

Appendix 2
Fleet Lists

Key to abbreviations: C/No.= Construction number; lsd = leased; opby = operated by; opf = operated for; rtl = return to lessor; std = stored; pwfu = permanently withdrawn from use

Sources
airfleets.net
CAA G-INFO website
planelogger.com
planespotters.net

Aircraft type	C/No.	Registration	Date	Notes/Fate
Bristol 175 Britannia 307F	12921	G-ANCE	Nov 1973–May 1974	to Aer Turas
Bristol 175 Britannia 308F	12922	G-ANCF	Dec 1968–Dec 1975	to African Safari Airways
Bristol 175 Britannia 309	12924	G-ANCH	Oct 1968–Apr 1972	to Ghana Airways
Bristol 175 Britannia 312	13238	G-AOVG	Oct 1969–Jan 1974	pwfu
	12925	G-AOVH	Apr 1968–May 1972	pwfu
	12926	G-AOVI	Mar 1968–May 1972	pwfu
	13420	G-AOVL	Mar 1969–May 1972	pwfu
	13422	G-AOVN	Aug 1969–Nov 1973	pwfu
	13427	G-AOVT	May 1969–Oct 1974	preserved at Duxford IWM
Boeing 707-100	17632	G-BFMI	Mar 1978–Jan 1979	to Cyprus Airways
	18054	G-BGCT	Dec 1978–Dec 1979	to Cyprus Airways
	17640	G-BHOX	Mar 1980–Dec 1980	to Air Malta
	17651	G-BHOY	Mar 1980–May 1980	to Air Malta
Boeing 707-355C	19664	G-AXRS	Apr 1981–Dec 1981	to Okada Airlines
Boeing 720B	18381	G-AZFB	Nov 1971–Mar 1983	lsd to Iraqi Airways (Aug–Nov 1974), Garuda Indonesian (Dec 1975–Jan 1976), Cyprus Airways (Jul 1977); to Jet Charter Service
	18382	G-AZKM	Jan 1972–Apr 1983	to Jet Charter Service
	18383	G-AZNX	March 1972–Mar 1983	to Jet Charter Service
	18792	G-BBZG	Mar 1974–Dec 1975	to Maersk Air

Aircraft type	C/No.	Registration	Date	Notes/Fate
	18014	G-BCBA	Mar 1977–Jan 1978; May 1978–Sep 1979; Jan 1980–Oct 1981	lsd to Cyprus Airways (Jan 1978–May 1978), Royal Air Maroc (Sep 1979–Jan 1980); to Maof Airlines
	18013	G-BCBB	Jan 1978–May 1978; Aug 1978–Oct 1981	lsd to Cyprus Airways (May 1978–Aug 1978); to Maof Airlines
	18421	G-BHGE	Nov 1979–Jul 1981	to Conair
BAC 1-11 500	186	G-AWWZ	Nov 1975–Oct 1985	to British Island Airways
	198	G-BCXR	Mar 1975–Mar 1983	to Dan-Air
	204	G-BCWG	Feb 1975–Oct 1976	to BAC
	201	G-AXMG	Oct 1976–May 1985	to British Island Airways
Boeing 737-200	22071	G-BJSO	Dec 1981–Oct 1983; Apr 1984–May 1984	rtl
	22416	G-BMON	Oct 1980-Dec 1985; Apr 1986-Dec 1986; May 1987-Dec 1987	lsd to Pacific Western (Dec 1985–Apr 1986; Dec 1986-May 1987), Canadian Airlines Int. (Dec 1987–Apr 1988); rtl
	22415	G-DFUB	Sep 1980–Nov 1984; Apr 1985–Dec 1986; Apr 1987–Jan 1988	lsd to Midway Express (Nov 1984–Apr 1985; Dec 1986–Apr 1987); rtl
	22762	G-DGDP	Mar 1982–Nov 1983; May 1984–Nov 1984; May 1985–Oct 1985	lsd to Pacific Western (Nov 1983–May 1984; Nov 1984–May 1985; Oct 1985–Apr 1986); to Canadian Pacific Airlines
	22761	G-DWHH	Mar 1982–Nov 1983; May 1984–Nov 1984; May 1985–Oct 1985; Apr 1986–Dec 1986	lsd to Pacific Western (Nov 1983–May 1984; Nov 1984–May 1985; Oct 1985–Apr 1986); to Canadian Pacific Airlines
	22368	G-GPAA	May 1984–Nov 1984	rtl
	21839	OO-SBS	May–June 1986	lsd Sobelair
Boeing 737-300	23827	G-BNXW	Oct 1987–Oct 1988	rtl
	24462	G-BWJA	Apr 1996–May 1997	rtl
	23495	G-DHSW	Mar 1986–Nov 1986; Apr 1987–Nov 1987; Apr 1988–Nov 1988; Apr–1989–Nov 1989; Mar 1990–Mar 1994	lsd to Pacific Western (Nov 1986–Apr 1987), Canadian Airlines Int. (Nov 1987–Apr 1988; Nov 1988–Apr 1989), Aviateca (Nov 1989–Mar 1990); opf Euroberlin (Apr 1990–Mar 1994); rtl

Aircraft type	C/No.	Registration	Date	Notes/Fate
	24237	G-EURP	Oct 1988–Oct 1990	to Germania
	23497	G-MONF	May 1986–Nov 1986; Apr 1987–Nov 1987; Apr 1988–Nov 1988; Apr 1989–Nov 1989; Mar 1990–Oct 1994	lsd to Pacific Western (Nov 1986–Apr 1987), Canadian Airlines Int. (Nov 1987–Apr 1988; Nov 1988–Apr 1989), Aviateca (nov 1989–Mar 1990); opf Euroberlin (Nov 1990–Dec 1990; May 1991–Oct 1994); rtl
	23498	G-MONG	May 1986–Nov 1987; Apr 1988–Oct 1988; Apr 1989–Apr 1995; Oct 1995–May 1996	lsd to Canadian Airlines Int. (Nov 1987–Apr 1988; Oct 1988–Apr 1989); opf Euroberlin (Apr 1990–Nov 1990; Nov 1991–Oct 1994); rtl
	23685	G-MONH	Mar 1987–Apr 1995	opf Euroberlin (Nov 1988–Apr 1995); rtl
	24255	G-MONL	Oct 1988–Dec 1991	opf Euroberlin (Nov 1988–Dec 1991); rtl
	24256	G-MONM	Nov 1988–Jan 1994	opf Euroberlin (Nov 1988–Apr 1991); rtl
	24029	G-MONN	Oct 1988–Nov 1993	opf Euroberlin (Nov 1988–Nov 1993); rtl
	24028	G-MONP	Oct 1988–May 1989; Apr 1990–Mar 1995	lsd to Inter European (May 1989-Apr 1990); opf Euroberlin (Oct 1990; Mar 1993-Mar 1995); rtl
	24026	G-MONT	Oct 1990–May 1991	opf Euroberlin (Oct 1990-May 1991); rtl
	24025	G-MONU	Oct 1990–Apr 1992	opf Euroberlin (Oct 1990-Apr 1992); rtl
	25033	G-MONV	Apr 1991–Apr 1996	rtl
Boeing 737-800	40874	G-ZBAV	May 2017–Oct 2017	lsd from Pegasus Airlines; rtl
Boeing 757-200	26151	EI-MON	May 2002–Oct 2002	lsd from Titan Airways
	23770	G-DAJB	Mar 1987–Nov 2014	to Icelandair
	23895	G-DRJC	May 1987–Apr 1988; Apr 1989–Nov 1989; Apr 1990–Mar 1993	lsd to British Airways (Apr 1988–Apr 1989); rtl
	24368	G-MCKE	Mar 1989–Nov 1996	rtl
	22780	G-MONB	Mar 1983–Dec 1995; Mar 1996–Nov 2008	lsd to Dinar Lineas Aereas (Dec 1995–Mar 1996); to FedEx

Aircraft type	C/No.	Registration	Date	Notes/Fate
	22781	G-MONC	Apr 1983–Nov 1988; Mar 1989–Apr 1990; Mar 1992–May 1996; Apr 1999–Nov 2008	lsd to Linas Aereas Hispania (Nov 1988–Mar 1989), Condor (Apr 1990–Mar 1992), Air Holland (May 1996–Apr 1999); pwfu
	22960	G-MOND	May 1983–Nov 1989; May 1992–Jan 2009	opf Australian Airlines (Nov 1989–Mar 1990); lsd to Condor (Apr 1990–May 1992); pwfu
	23293	G-MONE	Mar 1985–Nov 2008	to FedEx
	24104	G-MONJ	Apr 1988–Dec 1999; Mar 2000–Nov 2014	lsd to Spanair (Dec 1999–Mar 2000); pwfu
	24105	G-MONK	Apr 1988–Dec 1998; Mar 1999–Dec 1999; Mar 2000–Nov 2014	lsd to Dinar Lineas Aereas (Dec 1998–Mar 1999; Dec 1999–Mar 2020); to Icelandair
Boeing 767-31	28865	G-DIMB	Apr 2005–Mar 2010	lsd from MyTravel
Lockheed L-1011-1 Tristar	1051	TF-ABU	May 1998–Oct 1998	pwfu
McDonnell Douglas DC-10-30	48266	G-DMCA	Mar 1996–Oct 2001	pwfu
McDonnell Douglas MD-11	48519	N273WA	May 1998–Aug 1998	lsd from World Airways
	48743	N277WA	Aug 1998–Nov 1998	lsd from World Airways
Airbus A300B4-605R	604	G-MAJS	Apr 1991–Jan 2014	pwfu
	540	G-MONR	Mar 1990–Nov 1990; Jan 1992–Nov 2012	lsd to Compass Airlines (Nov 1990–Jan 1992); pwfu
	556	G-MONS	Apr 1990–Nov 1990; Feb 1992–Nov 2009; Dec 2009–Nov 2013	lsd to Compass Airlines (Nov 1990–Feb 1992), EgyptAir (Nov 2009–Dec 2009); pwfu
	605	G-OJMR	May 1991–Apr 2014	wfu
Airbus A320-200	391	G-MONW	Feb 1993–Dec 2004	to Tunisair
	392	G-MONX	Mar 1993–Nov 2013	rtl
	279	G-MONY	Jan 1993–Oct 1993; Apr 1994–Oct 1994; Apr 1995–Dec 1995; Mar 1996–May 1999	lsd to Canada 3000 Airlines (Oct 1993–Apr 1994; Oct 1994–Apr 1995; Dec 1995–Mar 1996); rtl
	379	G-MPCD	Mar 1994–Oct 1994; May 1995–Oct 1995; May 1996–Oct 1996; May 1997–Oct 1997; Apr 1998–Dec 2000; Apr 2001–Nov 2012	lsd to Skyservice Airlines (Oct 1994–May 1995; Oct 1995–May 1996; Oct 1996–May 1997; Oct 1997–Apr 1998), Canada 3000 Airlines (Dec 2000–Apr 2001); rtl

Aircraft type	C/No.	Registration	Date	Notes/Fate
	1081	G-MRJK	Apr 2005–Nov 2015	rtl
	422	G-OZBA	Mar 1994–May 1999	rtl
	389	G-OZBB	Mar 1994–Nov 1994; May 1995–Nov 1995; May 1996–Nov 1996; May 1997–Nov 1997; Apr 1998–Nov 1998; Apr 1999–Dec 1999; Apr 2000–Dec 2000; Apr 2001–Dec 2002; Apr 2003–Nov 2013	lsd to Skyservice Airlines (Nov 1994–May 1995; Nov 1995–May 1996; Nov 1996–May 1997; Nov 1997–Apr 1998; Nov 1998–Apr 1999), Airtours International (Dec 1999–Apr 2000), Canada 3000 Airlines (Dec 2000–Apr 2001), Zoom Airlines (Dec 2002–Apr 2003); wfu
	446	G-OZBJ	Oct 1993–Dec 1998; Apr 1999–Nov 1999; Apr 2000–Dec 2000; Apr 2001–Mar 2002; Feb 2005–Mar 2008	lsd to Skyservice USA (Dec 1998–Apr 1999; Nov 1999–Apr 2000; Dec 2000–Apr 2001); rtl
	1370	G-OZBK	Apr 2005–Nov 2014	rtl
	1571	G-OZBW	Mar 2012–Oct 2017	rtl
	1637	G-OZBX	Mar 2012–Oct 2017	rtl
	1320	G-OZBY	Jan 2013–Oct 2017	rtl
	5526	G-ZBAA	Mar 2013–Jan 2015	rtl
	5581	G-ZBAB	Apr 2013–Mar 2015	rtl
	1413	G-ZBAH	Jun 2013–Oct 2017	rtl
	1605	G-ZBAP	Feb 2014–Oct 2017	rtl
	2142	G-ZBAR	Apr 2014–Oct 2017	rtl
	6550	G-ZBAS	Apr 2015–Oct 2017	rtl
	3278	G-ZBAT	Dec 2015–Oct 2017	rtl
	3293	G-ZBAU	Apr 2016–Oct 2017	rtl
	1823	YL-LCP	May 2016–Oct 2016; May 2017–Oct 2017	wet lsd from SmartLynx
Airbus A321-231	983	G-MARA	Mar 1999–Oct 2017	rtl
	1015	G-OJEG	May 1999–Oct 2017	rtl
	633	G-OZBC	Apr 1997–May 2000	rtl
	1202	G-OZBD	Apr 2000–May 2003	rtl
	1707	G-OZBE	Mar 2002–Oct 2017	rtl
	1763	G-OZBF	Jun 2002–Oct 2017	rtl
	1941	G-OZBG	Mar 2003–Oct 2017	rtl
	2105	G-OZBH	Mar 2004–Oct 2017	rtl
	2234	G-OZBI	Jun 2004–Oct 2017	rtl
	864	G-OZBL	May 2006–Oct 2017	rtl

Aircraft type	C/No.	Registration	Date	Notes/Fate
	1045	G-OZBM	Mar 2007–Oct 2017	rtl
	1153	G-OZBN	Apr 2007–Oct 2017	rtl
	1207	G-OZBO	May 2007–Oct 2017	rtl
	1433	G-OZBP	Feb 2008–Nov 2014	rtl
	1794	G-OZBR	Apr 2008–Oct 2017	rtl
	1428	G-OZBS	Aug 2008–Dec 2014	rtl
	3546	G-OZBT	Feb 2009–Oct 2017	rtl
	3575	G-OZBU	Mar 2009–Oct 2017	rtl
	1421	G-OZBZ	Apr 2013–Oct 2017	rtl
	5582	G-ZBAD	May 2013–Oct 2017	rtl
	5606	G-ZBAE	May 2013–Oct 2017	rtl
	2730	G-ZBAF	Apr 2013–Oct 2017	rtl
	2793	G-ZBAG	Apr 2013–Oct 2017	rtl
	2553	G-ZBAI	Mar 2014–Oct 2017	rtl
	2610	G-ZBAJ	Apr 2014–Oct 2017	rtl
	3458	G-ZBAK	Apr 2014–Oct 2017	rtl
	3522	G-ZBAL	May 2014–Oct 2017	rtl
	6059	G-ZBAM	Apr 2014–Oct 2017	rtl
	6126	G-ZBAO	May 2014–Oct 2017	rtl
Airbus A330-243	265	G-EOMA	Apr 1999–Sep 2011; Dec 2011–Sep 2012; Dec 2012–Apr 2015	rtl
	261	G-SMAN	Mar 1999–Oct 2010; Dec 2010–Sep 2013; Nov 2013–Apr 2015	rtl

Appendix 3

Monarch Airlines Passenger Numbers 1968–2017

Source
Civil Aviation Authority (CAA)

	Scheduled passengers	Charter passengers	Total passengers	% Scheduled passengers	% Charter passengers
1968		122,873	122,873	0.0	100.0
1969		268,938	268,938	0.0	100.0
1970		295,888	295,888	0.0	100.0
1971		443,646	443,646	0.0	100.0
1972		529,021	529,021	0.0	100.0
1973		605,667	605,667	0.0	100.0
1974		505,930	505,930	0.0	100.0
1975		778,690	778,690	0.0	100.0
1976		731,972	731,972	0.0	100.0
1977		795,097	795,097	0.0	100.0
1978		946,621	946,621	0.0	100.0
1979		1,127,115	1,127,115	0.0	100.0
1980		1,086,519	1,086,519	0.0	100.0
1981		1,118,655	1,118,655	0.0	100.0
1982		1,151,392	1,151,392	0.0	100.0
1983		1,233,434	1,233,434	0.0	100.0
1984		1,494,387	1,494,387	0.0	100.0
1985		1,539,013	1,539,013	0.0	100.0
1986	9,020	1,971,156	1,980,176	0.5	99.5
1987	26,206	2,392,946	2,419,152	1.1	98.9
1988	24,646	2,429,120	2,453,766	1.0	99.0
1989	87,590	2,226,754	2,314,344	3.8	96.2
1990	105,037	2,355,489	2,460,526	4.3	95.7

	Scheduled passengers	Charter passengers	Total passengers	% Scheduled passengers	% Charter passengers
1991	87,312	2,168,320	2,255,632	3.9	96.1
1992	111,421	3,076,690	3,188,111	3.5	96.5
1993	138,212	3,621,837	3,760,049	3.7	96.3
1994	170,264	4,370,209	4,540,473	3.7	96.3
1995	189,979	4,326,199	4,516,178	4.2	95.8
1996	206,887	4,340,637	4,547,524	4.5	95.5
1997	246,576	4,286,796	4,533,372	5.4	94.6
1998	291,881	4,280,845	4,572,726	6.4	93.6
1999	334,783	4,481,477	4,816,260	7.0	93.0
2000	480,412	4,416,041	4,896,453	9.8	90.2
2001	620,876	4,092,344	4,713,220	13.2	86.8
2002	758,324	3,791,318	4,549,642	16.7	83.3
2003	1,322,572	3,303,262	4,625,834	28.6	71.4
2004	1,889,552	3,136,687	5,026,239	37.6	62.4
2005	2,558,218	2,794,378	5,352,596	47.8	52.2
2006	3,134,230	2,654,004	5,788,234	54.1	45.9
2007	3,625,732	2,521,233	6,146,965	59.0	41.0
2008	3,870,298	2,630,528	6,500,826	59.5	40.5
2009	3,668,528	2,453,557	6,122,085	59.9	40.1
2010	3,691,355	2,103,347	5,794,702	63.7	36.3
2011	4,541,172	1,391,291	5,932,463	76.5	23.5
2012	5,355,252	943,935	6,299,187	85.0	15.0
2013	6,032,879	788,789	6,821,668	88.4	11.6
2014	6,269,624	757,956	7,027,580	89.2	10.8
2015	5,496,455	226,780	5,723,235	96.0	4.0
2016	5,434,081	0	5,434,081	100.0	0.0
2017	3,403,637	0	3,403,637	100.0	0.0

Bibliography

Books
Bray, Roger and Raitz, Vladimir, *Flight to the Sun: The Story of the Holiday Revolution*, Continuum (2001)
Calder, Simon, *No Frills: The Truth Behind the Low-Cost Revolution in the Skies*, Virgin Books (2003)
Falconer, Jonathan, *Modern Civil Airliners*, JJN Publishing (2021)
Halford-MacLeod, Guy, *British Airlines Volume Three: 1964 to Deregulation*, The History Press (2010)
Merton Jones, Anthony C, *British Independent Airlines 1946–1976*, The Aviation Hobby Shop (2000)
Woodley, Charles, *Flying To The Sun*, The History Press (2016)
Wragg, David, *The World's Major Airlines* (2nd Edition), Sutton Publishing (2007)

Reports
Annual Report and Financial Statements of Monarch Holdings plc, 1999–2016

Magazines
Issues of:
Air International, Key Publishing Ltd
Aircraft Illustrated, Ian Allan Publishing
Airliner World, Key Publishing Ltd
Air Pictorial, Cheiron Press Ltd
Jets Monthly, Kelsey Publishing/Key Publishing Ltd
Propliner magazine

Electronic media
Wickstead, Maurice J, *Airlines of the British Isles since 1919*, Air-Britain (Historians) Ltd (2014)

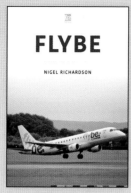
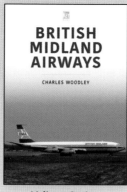
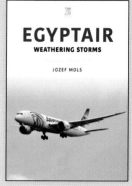

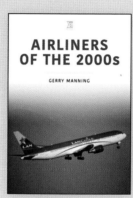